To Miss Rahman

A. Sanverdi

Ibrehim's dad.

Human Rights and Democracy in
International Relations:
Turkey and the EC 1980-1990

GW00691436

Dr. Ahmet Sanverdi

ISBN: 978-184426-748-2

To My Dear Parents

CONTENTS

ABSTRACT

Although there were some claims against particular states at international level regarding human rights violations against their citizens in the early 20th century from a historical point of view it can be claimed that the emergence of human rights on to the world stage in the context of international relations became a reality only in the second half of the 20th century after a disastrous war and humanitarian catastrophes. Despite the millions of deaths and committed genocide and widely committed crimes against humanity the concept largely that of sovereign states and its citizens stayed in tact until the end of the cold war in the late 1980s.

The problem can be identified in the essence of the international relations, which are based on the relations between sovereign states and sovereign territories. Thus the literature concerning with international relations generally tend to draw attention to the tension between the international community based on sovereign states and the moral obligations to which policy-makers cannot be indifferent in the way in which those states tend to treat their citizens. Additionally, strategic considerations in the cold war period had also influenced or even shaped the great powers' policies towards the human rights and democratic issues.

This study first looks at the gradual globalization of human rights and democracy in the international relations then as a casework examines the relations between the EU (as it was called by then the European Community) and Turkey with particular reference to human rights and democracy. In the 1980s particularly after the 1980 military coup the issues of human rights and democracy became the main source of tension in the relations between Turkey and the EC. However, despite the importance of human rights and democracy in the EU-Turkish relations between 1980 and 1990 and even in the following years, there are not many comprehensive studies about the issues and their implications in EU-Turkish relations or their significant role in the whole democratization process in Turkey. Instead, most of the literature and the academic studies focus on the economic and strategic issues and their significance in the relationship. The Greek factor and the Cyprus question have also gained in importance and have been dealt with comprehensively in recent years both by the European and Turkish academics. This study aims to contribute to fill a gap by providing an overall understanding of the issues of human rights and democracy and their relevance and implications in EU-Turkish relations between 1980 and 1990 as well as explaining the steady increase importance of human rights and democracy in the international relations.

Two fundamental principles have been identified as the determining factors of the relations between the EC and Turkey: Turkey's receptive response to the European pressure and the Community's pressure policy towards Turkey. The first one related to Turkey's strong ideological, (self-identification with Europe) economic, political and military linkages with Europe and its aspiration to membership of the EC. This was the fundamental source of Turkey's receptive and responsive relationship with the EC thorough the period. The second was the critical European stance and its implementation in a policy that employed political, economic and diplomatic approaches. This was in line with the EC's internal and international political developments towards the globalization of the human rights issues. Similar frameworks between states and international or intergovernmental organizations have been seen in different quarters of the World particularly after the collapse of the cold war. The European responses to the military regime between 1980 and 1983, and to the civilian governments between 1983 and 1990, have been assessed in a critical and chronological framework with analytical argument on one hand and evidence on the other. It is suggested that the whole relationship in these periods was marked by various attempts by the EC to put constraints on Turkey and that Ankara's responses to the EC's approach ended up in a working consultative relationship.

1) Introduction

Human rights and democratic issues in international relations have always been problematic. It developed gradually and only became a reality in the recent decades. In this study, I will first examine the internationalisation of human rights issues and the evolution of human rights policy in the EEC/EC foreign relations and the relevance to the relations between the EC and Turkey. After this, I move to examine the actual human rights and democracy issues in the relations between the EC and Turkey. It will be argued that neither the EEC nor the member states had an active human rights policy in their foreign agendas until the late 1970s. It is also argued that the emergence of an active human rights policy in the EEC foreign relations was not a rapid change of policy but was a gradual development, which had two main dimensions; internal and external. These directly related to the increase of human rights awareness in the European constituencies and to international developments in 1970s and 1980 in favour of the inclusion of the issues of human rights and democracy into the foreign policy agenda. As will be examined, American influence on European common strategic and security considerations played a major role in the 1970s and 1980s, but, more importantly, the collapse of the Communist Bloc and democratic developments in the Eastern European countries played a positive role in this process. As will be seen the focus of this study will be on human rights and democracy in the relations between the EU and Turkey during both the military regime (1980-1983) and civilian rule (1983-1990). This is a classical example of the development of the EU policy in its international relations which later became EU official stand in its international relations. It will be argued that the strategic and security considerations of the EC, particularly in the early years of the military regime, overlapped with the principle of the promotion and protection of human rights and democracy. Thus the relations between the EC and Turkey in the early period of the military regime were not significantly affected by Turkey's human rights record or lack of democracy. However, after 1981 the EC changed its policy towards Turkey and gradually adopted a more critical stance, which brought Turkey's internal affairs into its foreign relations with the EC.

The issues of human rights and democracy have particularly become problematic and the center of tensions in international relations after World War II. The problem can be identified in the essence of the international relations, which are based on the relations between sovereign states and sovereign territories. Thus the literature concerning with international relations generally tend to draw attention to the tension between the international community based on sovereign states and the moral obligations to which policy-makers cannot be indifferent in the way in which those states tend to treat their citizens. This tension is particularly obvious in a state - centric approach to international law, which ascribes rights and obligations to states as sovereign entities. (1) This stance is bound to be problematic. When such an approach is adopted, it leaves only a limited space for any government or any non-governmental international organization to raise a particular state's human rights record as a legitimate concern in their relations. On the other hand, the same approach creates space for the accused states to avoid their obligations for as Vincent argues human rights and foreign policy have different constituencies. According to Vincent, "the society of all human kind stands in contrast to the society of states. Giving this condition, foreign-policy makers would generally tend either to reflect a reluctance to concern themselves with human rights issues or to use them as a means of leverage in relations with their counterparts". (2)

However, the European Community policy-making process in the area of human rights and democracy differs from the above classical definitions. The policy-making process of the Community in its essence is different from that of both nation-states and intergovernmental organizations. (3) First, the sources of the human rights policy itself and the input into the policy - making process comes from both supranational and national levels. Therefore, the process is more protracted than that of nation states but more dynamic and comprehensive than that of intergovernmental organizations. Second, the influence of social assertiveness on policy outcomes is more pronounced than what can be expected in intergovernmental organizations, but less direct than can be observed in nation-states. (4) Another important aspect of the Community's policy- making process regarding the human rights policy is that it is integrated into a complex procedural structure that has three main partners, the Commission, the Council and the European Parliament and the influence of individual member-states on them.

As will be examined, the policy-making bodies have not always agreed on the type or the degree of the assertiveness of human rights policy with regard to non-EC countries. This either led to compromise, which mostly led to adopting a new policy or suspension of the suggested policy. Moreover, the policy makingbodies, as is the case in the Turkey-EC relations, often took different stances against alleged human rights abuses. For example, while the EP took a critical stance and asked the Community to suspend all relations with Turkey, the other two bodies were keen to develop a consultative co-operative relationship with Turkey after 1980 military coup. Therefore, as will be shown, the Community's initial approach to the military regime was as soft as it could be.

This was, of course, due to strategic concerns in the region and Turkey's importance in the Western military alliance and its active role in NATO.

However, after 1981 the Community's approach to the military regime changed. In order to force the military rulers to return to civilian rule the EC took numerous diplomatic, political and economic measures. The EC influenced the military rulers to return to civilian rule but could not affect the democratization processes and political developments prior to general elections in 1983. Therefore, the EC did not change its stance against Turkey and continued to use diplomatic, economic and political means for further democratization in Turkey. On the other hand, the Ankara government faced conflicting pressures between introducing reforms so to normalize the relations with the EC and struggling with the military establishment and conservative forces in the country. As a result of this, the Ozal government tried to deal with the EC in a form of consultative and co-operative relationship. It introduced reforms in line with European expectations but had to do this gradually in order not to upset conservative forces and the military establishment in the country.

2) The Emergence of Human Rights on to the World Stage in the 20 century

From a historical perspective one can claim that the emergence of human rights on to the world stage in the context of international relations became a reality only in the second half of the 20th century. Yet the concept largely that of sovereign states and its citizens until the end of the cold war in the late 1980s.

Prior to the Universal Declaration of Human Rights, two significant attempts had been made to establish a principle of agreement at international level recognising the equality of individuals. The first attempt was made after the First World War in 1919. During the preparation of the League of Nations Covenant the Japanese delegation formally proposed that the Covenant should contain that "...the High Contracting parties agree to accord, as soon as possible, to all alien nationals of member-states, equal and just treatment in every respect, making no distinction, either in law or in fact, on account of their race and nationality". (5) Despite its limited scope the proposal was rejected particularly because of opposition from Britain. (6) A milder proposal was submitted by the Japanese but this was also rejected. The main concern according to the British delegate, Lord Robert Cecil, was that the Japanese proposal "opened the door to serious controversy and to interference in the domestic affairs of states members of the League". (7)

The second proposal came in 1933 after a complaint launched by a German citizen of Jewish origin, Franz Bernheim, to the Council of the League of Nations about the breaches by Germany of the

German - Polish Treaty of 1922. The rejection this time came from the German delegate who claimed that "the Jewish citizen had no right to sue the German government to the Council of the League. On the other hand, Polish and French delegates advocated that a minimum of rights must be guaranteed to every human being, whatever his race, religion or mother tongue."(8) Despite the German opposition the Council appointed a commission to investigate the case. Finally, the commission found the German Government guilty of wrong doing and adopted a report asking the German Government to bring the violations to an end. However, as we know German discrimination against the Jewish people did not stop there. In the following days, the French delegate made a proposal regarding minority rights, and specifically the right of the Jewish minority in Germany. All other members accepted the proposal but because of German veto the proposal was not accepted. (9) The German delegate claimed that Jewish problem was Germany's internal concern. Furthermore, three days later on 14 October 1933 the German Government announced its withdrawal from the League on the grounds that Germany was not treated equally to the other nations.

As is clearly demonstrated by the above examples in the 1930s, any international concern regarding human rights by another state or an international organisation was regarded as external interference in domestic issues. As we know, only a few years later Germany started the most bloody and destructive war in recorded history. During the war Nazi forces not only violated human rights but also carried out ethnic cleansing and committed atrocities against minorities of their country and others. After the War human rights violations and particularly atrocities committed by Germans against the Jewish people became to the attention of the international community, which paved way for the gradual globalisation of human rights in the following decades.

Following the War, two fundamental principles were established in the context of international relations and incorporated into the United Nations Charter the right of people to self-determination (which was originally advocated by Lenin following the First World War) and human rights for all. However, the most important breakthrough regarding human rights came in 1948 with the proclamation of the Universal Declaration of Human Rights, which was followed in 1966 by two more United Nations Covenants on human rights. (10) Encouraged by "the right of people to self determination" many former colonies gained their independence. As a result of this, following the World War Two, human rights and democratic principles have been gradually incorporated into the foreign policy agendas of the major international political powers and organisations. Although there was no swift change these developments formed the bases for the later internationalisation of human rights and democratic principles. However, these positive developments did not change the fundamental structure of international relations, which was based on independent states and their sovereignty over their territory and citizens until the late 1980s. Nevertheless, after the collapse of the Soviet Bloc, the principle of protection and promotion of human rights and democracy has widely been accepted as a legitimate concern of the international community.

The international responses to the Iraqi invasion of Kuwait, the ethnic cleansing in Bosnia, the human catastrophe in Kosovo and East Timor resulted from the accumulation of the above policy. To this end, as a response to the internationalisation of human rights and the emerging trend of the globalisation of world politics and economics the old concept of non-interventionism in domestic affairs of a sovereign state has (at least in practice) been re-defined to accommodate the new changes which transcend the national boundaries. This has resulted in a form of international action that promotes and protects human rights and democratic principles by diplomatic, political, economic and even military means.

Although these actions have been mostly led by the international powers, particularly the US, and have been based on wider economic and strategic considerations than just human rights causes, the authorisation of the UN has widely been used to legalise or legitimise external interventions in the domestic affairs of a sovereign state. This has usually been to the advantage of the US and/or other western states. The striking examples of such policies are the no-fly zone in Northern Iraq and military intervention in Kosovo where UN authorisations were obtained after the actual military actions were taken on the ground. Although it can be argued that UN has been used by aggressive forces as a puppet to legitimise their actions, it can still be asserted that international actors such as the UN, NATO, the EU and to some extent some regional organisations started to see themselves as having the will and legitimacy to take up human rights causes and their actions were largely supported by other players. This implies that the international promotion and protection of human rights now exists to at least some extent.

However, despite the above examples of successful international military interventions on humanitarian grounds in Bosnia, Kosova and East Timor, the international response to the similar or even worse human tragedies in some other parts of the world such as Chechenya, Karabag and Rwanda have not been in the same pattern as the above. This suggests that the state centric approach to world politics has not been totally changed. On the contrary the centre-piece of the state-centric approach as expressed in the UN Charter 2/7 is still operative in contemporary world politics, particularly when the strategic and economic interests of so called super-states are not in danger.

Nevertheless, human rights issues have now transcended the strict notion of non-interventionism as the ultimate norm to rule international relations. In the face of the changing structure of world economic and politics, the principle of non-interventionism, which is based on absolute state sovereignty in its domestic affairs, is largely changed. As a result of this it is now almost impossible to isolate a state's internal affairs from its foreign relations. This leads to a form of compulsory inter-communicative relations regarding the internal affairs with other sovereign states or international governmental and non-governmental organisations or face possible diplomatic, economic, political and/or military actions taken by third parties. As a result of this new international trend, national governments do not feel absolutely free to treat their citizens as they could in the past.

3) European States and Human Rights Policy

From a historical viewpoint, human rights or moral values have not played an important role in the foreign policies of the European states. As Dagi puts it ".... Europe did not have a political tradition based on historical commitment to an assertive foreign policy aimed at promoting human rights and democracy in the world". (11) Instead, throughout the 19 century and in the first half of the 20th century a balance of power politics was the core of the foreign policies of the major European countries. Although the French Revolution provided some ideological approaches to foreign policy to promote similar regimes in Europe, the fight for basic rights and freedoms remained local (12) and the idea of non-intervention in nation states' internal affairs prevailed in European politics until the late 1980s.

However, particularly after World War Two, the social and political history of Europe evolved towards a common political culture in which democracy, human rights, liberal economic policies and the right of individual constituted the core. The experience of Hitler's regime and its crimes against humanity in total disrespect for basic human rights had a significant impact on the evolution of a common political culture on the Continent. This experience made it clear that totalitarian regimes, such as fascist Hitler and Mussolini, represent a great danger not only for individual countries but also for the whole of Europe and its moral, political and economic values. These concerns led to the creation of a common policy in which not the only assertion but also the protection of the rights of individuals and minorities would be central at a European level. Historically, from the post World War Two onwards, human rights and democratic values have gradually gained a place on the foreign policy agenda of the Western European states. In this gradual development, the involvement of the US in European politics, particularly after World War Two, was another important factor in the growing Western European interest in human rights policy.

To this end the formation of the Council of Europe in 1949 was a corner stone in the political history of Europe in the 20th century. This followed with the Convention on Human Rights in 1950. Article 3 of the Convention prohibited torture and inhuman or degrading treatment or punishment. The Convention was opened for signature in Rome on 4 November 1950 and entered into force in September 1953. The object of the Convention was to take the first steps for the collective enforcement of certain of the rights stated in the United Nations Universal Declaration of Human Rights of 1948. In addition to laying down a catalogue of civil and political rights and freedoms, the Convention set up a system of enforcement of the obligations entered into by Contracting States. Three institutions were entrusted with this responsibility: the European Commission of Human Rights, (set up in 1954) the European Court of Human Rights (13) and the Committee of Ministers of the Council of Europe. Members of the Council of Europe also signed the European Convention for the Prevention of Torture and Inhuman or Degrading Treatment or Punishment on 26 June 1987, which became effective on 1 February 1989. This was followed by an additional protocol on 4 November 1993. (14)

4) The European Community's human rights policy and its evolution: internal and external factors

The evolution of the European Community's human-rights policy can be observed in its founding agreement and later historical developments. Although the Treaty of Rome does not mention human rights either in internal relations or international affairs, gradually the Community throughout its historical development has established a strong sense of the importance of protecting and promoting human rights and democracy both internally and internationally. Therefore, the European Community's human-rights policy can be characterized by two main dimensions.

The internal dimension is directly related to raising concerns and awareness about the human rights issues in the European constituencies, while the external dimension, is mainly related to the promotion and protection of human rights and democratic values in non- EC countries. This is the primary concern of this chapter with regard to Turkey.

To state it broadly, the Community's human rights policy has evolved as a result of prior change and the shift of national policies in the member states which was a response to the increasing human-rights awareness of the European constituents. This has been clearly observed from the early 1970s onwards. This fact supports the argument that the Community's external policy-making process was not formed in accordance with a sudden change or primarily set out ideological and political ideas but as a result of continuous and steady changes and convergence among national policies.

The external factors, particularly the US Government's influence, may also be added here. However, according to Ugur "the external influences were mediated through the dynamics of the state society relations into action and may or may not be conducive to policy harmonization or integration or integrated policy - making process at the Community level". (15) For example, the US human-rights policy towards the Eastern Bloc countries and the US attempts to influence the Community's human rights policy received different reactions from different member states. The Federal Republic of Germany and France signaled explicit disagreement with the negative implications of the US activism for detente in East - West European relations. Their concerns were that the US activism on human rights issues within the Soviet Bloc might provoke Soviet reactions that could jeopardize their commercial and political relations with the Soviet Union and other Warsaw Pact countries. (16) These considerations can be taken as an important factor in the reluctance of the Council and the member states in the 1970s and early 1980s to respond positively to the Parliament's various requests for a more active human rights stance in the Community's foreign policy. On the other hand, the British government, alongside the Benelux countries and Northern states, was willing to support an active human rights policy in line with the US position. However, in the absence of consensus among the member states the Community could not produce an active and critical human rights policy commitment in its foreign policy until the mid 1980s.

Above all, the EC's critical stance in the areas of human rights and democracy was hindered by the different agendas and priorities held by the member states and the Council on the one hand and the Commission and the Parliament on the other. This tension and the different priorities and policies between the main policy- making bodies of the Community have not always been resolved in favour of either institution. Instead, a compromise situation has been preferred most of the time. Nevertheless, in respect to human rights policy, particularly in relations with third countries, of which Turkey has been a prime example, the EP has predominantly influenced the Community agenda.

The European Union's human rights policy has evolved through two phases. The first phase, which was essentially inward looking, lasted until the early 1980s. The second phase has been more outward looking. In this phase, which is still ongoing, the Community has adopted an active human rights policy particularly in its relations with third countries. During the first phase, the EC's involvement in human rights issues was started off by internal developments to which the European Court of Justice had to respond. Starting from the mid 1960s, the court delivered judgments on various human rights cases and "referred to the constitutional traditions of the member states as considerations of fundamental relevance to its judgments". (17) Following this the European Parliament also started to raise its voice for an EC human rights agenda that would provide solutions for individuals, particularly those directly affected by Community legislation. (18) However, contrary to expectations the outcome of these initiatives was not very significant.

In terms of legislation and practice, the Copenhagen summit statement of 14th December 1973 was a turning point in the Community's history. In the declaration of the summit, the European identity was characterized as "..... upholding the principles of representative democracy and respect for human rights". (19) Another significant step was taken by the inter-institutional declaration of 1977 against racism and xenophobia. All these important steps were largely inward-looking and they did not have a great impact in the Community's human rights policy in its foreign relations.

However, during the second phase, the human rights policy of the EC became more outward looking as well as more active, critical and effective in its foreign policy. Starting with the publication of the Parliament Reports in 1983 onwards, the second half of the 1980s witnessed various developments. First, the Single European Act provided that human rights issues should be an essential element in the context of the Community's external relations. By the Single European Act the Parliament gained a greater power and right to have a vote on any enlargement. This strengthened the EP's position with regard to democracy and human rights issues, which have always been raised by the EP among the policy-making bodies of the Community. Secondly, a number of statements and joint declarations were made from 1986 onwards at various levels in which the link between external economic and political relations and human rights issues was made obvious and essential. (20) Third, for the first time in its history, the Community introduced human rights clauses into the Association Agreements with African Caribbean and Pacific (PCP) countries. Forth, European political Cooperation (EPC), in line with the Community, increased its activities in the field of human rights towards countries with poor human rights records. The list of countries regarded by the Community as having negative human rights records increased from 20 to 50 between 1981 - 1986 and to 150 in 1991. (21)

During the 1980s, the EC was challenged by some important international developments, which meant new requirements and policy changes in its external relations. The political and social developments in Eastern Europe, which led to the collapse of the Soviet bloc, brought democracy and human rights issues to the centre of EC relations with those countries. The EC's diplomatic responses to the political and social developments in the Eastern European countries was not only a shift from a low profile to a high profile human-rights policy but was also a signal of activism and commitment.

The first signal of this change came in 1988, when the German permanent representative at the United Nations made a joint declaration on behalf of the 12 member states. This declaration was not the first joint declaration that was made on behalf of the member states, but was notable for its contents and language, which were very different from those of previous joint declarations. The declaration called for "... improving and strengthening the working mechanism of the special rapporteurs, the working group on enforced or involuntary disappearance and the UNHR itself". (22) In the following years many more similar high-profile statements were made both at the ministerial and ambassadorial levels which clearly stated the Community's critical stance and activism regarding human rights and democratic issues in the former Soviet Bloc. (23) However, as is the case with some other countries such as Turkey, the Community's stand on the issues of human rights and democracy was not straightforward. First of all, the EC's interest in the human rights records of non-EC countries proved to be a short-term development. This was revealed in the November 1991 Paris summit of the CSCE and become even more apparent in the Helsinki II document. In this meeting the EC member states, in contrast to the US line, were concerned with security issues. As Amnesty International (AI) has pointed out "..... human rights had to fight for survival at Helsinki II".(24)

The evidence suggested that, although external factors had some influence on the EC's human-rights policy, the same external factors ironically led to a shift of attention away from human rights considerations towards concerns about security and other foreign policy priorities such as commercial and political links. For this reason I would argue that, the external factors have had vitally important effects on the policy-making bodies of the EC in the fields of human rights and democracy. To this end the most important factor has been the collapse of the Cold War and political developments in the Eastern Europe, which paved the way to a greater enlargement of the EC. However, it is impossible to deny the role of the internal factors in shaping the Community's active human rights policy.

The indications of the impact of internal factors on the Community's human-rights policy can be seen in both independent studies and in the Community documents. For instance, a case study which was undertaken in various EC countries in 1977 shows that about 70 to 80 per cent of the respondents in Germany and France supported the definition of an extensive catalogue of human rights that went beyond state - granted privileges. (25) Analysis of data on British and Italian attitudes in the same study reflected a similar result. The author of this study witnessed this kind of pressure on some MEP's when he interviewed them. For example, when Pauline Green (MEP for North London and leader of the Socialist group in the EP) was asked why her group was blocking the Customs Union Agreement with Turkey, she replied "Europe is a democratic society where human-rights and minority rights are highly respected." Above all she said, " we represent these European people who want to see at least some improvements in human rights practices in Turkey". (26) Similar trends were seen in a survey conducted by the Commission in 1989. Between 60 and 94 per cent of the respondents stated that human rights should be respected under all circumstances. Furthermore 48 per cent of the respondents claimed that the Community's human-rights policy was not adequately active. (27)

Such surveys alone, of course, cannot be taken as a conclusive proof of the impact of domestic factors on the emergence and formation of the EC's human rights policy. However, they can be taken as evidence to support the argument that the politicians of the EC countries and particularly the MEPs were faced with strong pro-human rights tendencies among the people, which formed an active front in various constituencies. These were often influenced by refugees and dissident immigrants most of whom have been active against human rights violations in their countries. These have played an important role in mobilizing European opinion on the promotion of human rights and democracy in non-EC countries. Ironically the same factors have mobilized far right, racist and fascist movements in the member-states. Whatever the reason, European politicians could not ignore the increasing active pro-human rights tendencies of the European electorate. For example, in his report Ken Coates indicated that the Parliament's high level of activity in the area of human rights was "... largely a response to the concerns of the electorate, and the inter-nationalization human-rights movement, which is essentially sustained by the concerns of individual citizens". (28) Moreover, the documents showed that the link between Constituency's expectations and attitudes and the Community's human-rights policy have not been limited to the EP's statements only. Evidence indicates that almost all the Council declarations concerning human rights outside the Community have contained statements appealing to domestic expectations. (29) The above analysis would suggest that the Community's human-rights policy was initiated as a result of public expectations and increasing awareness of human rights in the European constituencies and developed in line with the gradual globalization of human rights issues, which in combination with the internal factors, shaped the Community's human rights policy particularly regard to non-EC countries.

However, with regard to the context of forming a human rights policy and particularly raising the issues of human rights and democracy and the Community's relations with third countries, the Parliament has always been ahead of the Commission and the Council. The Parliament has always been the main source of the policy-making process in relation to human rights and influenced the other two parties. Comparisons of the Parliament's activism in the content and timing of its resolutions with policy announcements made by the Council or the Commission provide clear evidence to this effect. For example, the first inter institutional declaration of April 1977 was largely influenced by the EP. The inclusion of references to human rights into the Lome conventions was also influenced by the Parliament. (30) The first Parliament recommendation to this effect was made in 1983 and such references were included in Lome III in 1985 as general statements and as binding articles in Lome IV of December 1989. Similarly, the call for the incorporation of human rights as an element of external relations was made by the Parliament in its resolution of 17 May, 1983. The EP has stated in almost all its resolutions that expressions of concern about the violation of human rights cannot be considered as interference in domestic affairs. This principle was only made public in the Foreign Minister's statement of 21 July 1986 and by the European Council in its Luxembourg Declaration of 29 June 1991. (31)

The EP has also been ahead of the Council and the Commission in the institutionalization of the human rights policy process. For example, the EP first established a Working Group on human rights within its Political Affairs Committee in October 1980. This group was later upgraded to a Sub-Committee on Human Rights in 1984. The Parliament also requested the appointment of a Commissioner charged with human-rights issues in 1986. This request was not favored by the Council so it was not adopted but as a result of the parliament's pressure "Directorate F" within the general secretariat responsible for intergovernmental co-operation between the member states was created in May 1988. "Directorate F" was charged with the provision of a specialized service for the co-ordination of human rights policy among the member states. (32)

5) Human Rights and Democracy in the Relations between the EC and Turkey : 1980-1990

Turkey's relationship with the Community formally started in July 1959 with Turkey's application for membership, which led to the Association Agreement of Ankara signed in December 1963. Despite the military coup of 27 May 1960 and 12 March 1971 and widespread allegations of human-rights violations in the 1970s, the European Community started to pay attention to the human rights records of Turkey only after the 1980 military coup. Even though the early reaction of the EC to the military takeover was a mild one, later, the human rights and democracy issues became a dominant factor in Turkey's economic and political relations with the Community.

Community's early soft and passive stance to the military coup can be explained in the following terms. There were three main reasons for the Community's initial stance. The first, and most important reason was the fact that the member states had strategic considerations with regard to Turkey, which shaped the Community's policy towards Turkey at the time. The withdrawal of Greece from NATO's military command following the Cyprus conflict with Turkey in 1974 left Turkey as the only contributor to NATO in the region. The Russian invasion of Afghanistan in December 1979 and the Islamic revolution of 1979 in Iran also contributed to Western strategic considerations. The second cause was a co-existence of human rights violations in Turkey with political turmoil and increasing political violence, which led to about 20 deaths a-day. The escalation of terrorist activities in weak short-lived coalition governments overshadowed Turkey's human rights record. Despite the various records of Amnesty International (AI) on Turkey, the violations of human rights was seen as related to the short-lived weak coalition governments and the lack of democracy rather than to systematic human-rights violations. (33) Therefore, some argue that at the time European opinion was preoccupied with images of political turbulence in terrorist activities associated with a weak democracy rather than with systematic human rights violations. (34) However, I would suggest that the European passive human rights policy was in line with the American administration's human-rights policy, which was based on permissiveness towards friendly "authoritarian" governments, but active criticism against unfriendly "totalitarian" regimes. (35) The latter can be characterized as the Eastern Bloc countries, other communist countries, (i.e. Cuba, China, North Korea) and some other non-Communist but hostile regimes such as Iran and Libya. The former approach was used for allied and friendly countries such as Israel, Turkey, Chile and some military regimes in South America, Asia and Africa. The third important factor was the Community's general stand on human rights. At that period the Community's human rights policy was fundamentally inward looking. Therefore, in general terms, the Community did not have an active human rights policy in its external relations with third countries at the time and Turkey was a prime example of this lack.

The Community's overall human-rights policy vis-a-vis the Turkish military regime between 1980 and 1983 may be described as a series of attempts at striking a balance between its interests in maintaining a working relationship with a military regime and the need to reconcile strategic considerations, with the Community's emerging high-profile and active human-rights policy towards non-EC countries. The evolution of this policy can be examined in two phases. The first phase began with the military coup and ended with the first general elections in 1983. The second phase was between 1983-1990.

The first phase can be characterized by two main tendencies within the Community. First, the member states were generally in favor of a wait and see approach even though some of them were prepared to adopt a relatively more critical stance. On the other hand, the Parliament was in favour of a critical stance and an active policy towards Turkey and it did what it could, but its influence on the overall human-rights policy of the Community towards Turkey remained limited. This was mainly because of the differences between the governments of the member states and the very low levels of contact between the EP and the Turkish military regime particularly within the association framework.

The second phase can be divided into two periods. The first part was characterized by of the Parliament's determination not to recognize the newly elected civil Turkish government and the Parliament as legitimate representatives of Turkish people. To this end, the EP blocked the normalization of the EC relations with Turkey and did not activate the Joint Parliamentarian Committee (JPC) despite the Commission's positive approach towards Turkey. In this period the gap between the Parliament and the member states on Turkey was even wider and the EP became a main player in the relations between Turkey and the EC. This period ended with Turkey's application for full membership in April 1987. The second part of this phase was marked by a deterioration of the relations between Turkey and the EC despite the existence of a civilian government and its effort towards democratization in Turkey. Furthermore, there was a gradual emergence of consensus among the member states to see Turkey's human rights record as an obstacle for full-scale normalization of relations and especially full membership of the EC. It can be argued that, in this phase, the member states moved to a position, which was closer to that of the EP. More importantly, the Community took a more critical stance and specific issues such as the Kurdish question and specific clauses of Turkish laws and constitution were being discussed between the two parties. This period ended with the rejection of Turkey's application for full membership in December 1989.

6) The First Phase 1980 - 1983: the Military Regime and the EC

The first reaction of the Community to the military coup came from the Commission on 13 September 1980. In line with the Community's current human-rights policy the Commission's first response to the military coup was not an aggressive one. In fact, it was a very mild one in line with the US and some member states particularly Germany's, responses to the coup. The Commission statement was couched in general terms and did not include any specific recommendation. The Commission, stated that "... it is following the developments in Turkey with the greatest concern and the Community hopes to see that human rights will be fully respected."(36) The most important aspect of the statement was that it did not contain any indication about what implications the military coup would have for the future of the relations between the EC and Turkey.

The soft approach was also maintained in the statement of the foreign ministers on 15 September 1980. The foreign ministers of the member states expressed concern about the developments in Turkey and took note of the assurances given by the National Security Council (NSC) concerning the "rapid re-establishment of democratic institutions and observance of human rights." They stated that the foreign ministers were "...deeply anxious that those assurances were put into practice as soon as possible." (37) These statements were not only significant because of the contents but also because of their future implications of a wait and see policy stance.

As explained above, this stance mainly related to the member states' strategic considerations, which also shaped the human rights policy of the community.

In addition to the above considerations, the Junta's rhetoric, with its emphasis on saving Turkish democracy from disintegration in the face of political turmoil and the inability of the government to govern, were generally seen as genuine reasons for the military takeover both in Europe and at home. However, the above statements were unexpectedly soft even in the eyes of the Turkish military. Since the statements were couched in general terms and contained no condemnation or even strong language, they were welcomed by the military and were interpreted as European diplomatic approval of the new regime. (38) In fact, the statements were more reassurances to the new military regime that overthrew an elected civilian government than condemnations. The main reason was that the foreign ministers were convinced by the assurances given by the Junta that a rapid return to democracy would take place and human rights would be respected.

As a result, the foreign ministers of the member states decided there was no need to suspend the Association Agreement or the Fourth Financial Protocol providing Turkey with substantial economic aid (600 million ECU). Finally, the ministers decided to continue economic and political co-operation as normal and keep the association agreement alive. (39) This stance can be attributed to the strategic considerations explained above. Following the military coup, the consensus that emerged in the Community might be characterized as taking the NSC promises as given and using the Fourth Financial Protocol as a modest means of leverage to accelerate the return to civilian rule in ensuring respect for human rights. It can be argued that this was a compromise that first and foremost served the interest of some member states, which were anxious not to alienate Turkey in a period of instability in the region and push the new military regime away from the sphere of influence of the Community. While the Commission was in tune with the above compromise, it was difficult to incorporate the EP in this policy. The Parliament took a strong critical stance against the military regime.

The chairman of the EP delegation to the EC-Turkey Joint Parliamentary Committee (JPC) made a statement on 15 September and called for immediate steps towards the restoration of democratic institutions and a freeing of all political prisoners. The statement also insisted that Parliamentary democracy was "... a fundamental pre-condition for the full application of the EC-Turkey Association". (40) The Parliament discussed two resolutions in its plenary meeting of 17 September 1980. One was submitted by the Communist members who asked for an immediate suspension of relations between the EC and Turkey. The second was submitted by the Socialists, Christian Democrats and Liberals and was less critical in its demands. In close harmony with the Commission and the Council decisions and aware of the member states' and the Commission's position, the majority of the EP decided to adopt the second resolution. The resolution stated that "the current situation in Turkey was not only incompatible with Turkey's international binding commitments {such as those under the ECHR, but also with its association agreement with the community}. Suspension of relations would be considered if Turkey did not return to democracy as soon as possible."(41)

Although this particular resolution agreed, in general terms, with the core of the Council and Commission declarations, it was quite clear that the Parliament was ready to adopt a more critical stance and put more pressure on Turkey than the Commission and the Council. A number of MEPs spoke out and blamed both institutions for taking a soft approach towards the military coup. On the other hand, the Council and the Commission were adamant in their policy and tried hard to sell it to the MEPs. Speaking on behalf of the Council, Mr.Gaston Thorn tried to assure the EP by emphasizing the promises given by the leaders of the military regime and stating that the suspension of relations would not serve the interest of the Turkish people but those of the coup-makers. Therefore, the Commission believed that the best policy would be " to maintain the association relations with the anticipation that democracy would be restored as soon as possible."(42) This approach was, of course, unacceptable for many MEP's as well as leaving a question mark on the issue of whether democracy was a precondition for an association agreement. However, neither the Parliament's resistance nor the situation in Turkey had an immediate effect on the Commission and the Council. So, in the first year of the military regime, official relations between Turkey and the EC hardly deteriorated and scheduled businesses was carried out as normal. On the other hand, a fortnight after the military takeover on 1 October 1980, the Council of Europe held a meeting to discuss the new situation in Turkey. Interestingly, in that meeting the member states of the EC seemed to be prepared for a more critical stance against Turkey than they did in the EC. After intense discussions and despite Turkey's hard lobbying, the Council declared that Turkey "...cannot remain a member unless it returns to democracy as soon as possible."(43) Although this resolution was not as strong as was expected, the declaration indicates that member states of the EC were prepared to participate in a stronger critical action against Turkey in the Council of Europe and not in the EC. This can be taken as indication that the Community was reluctant to assign a high profile to its human rights policy towards third countries at the time. The difference of stance in the two bodies was also due to pressure in the Council of Europe from non-EC member states such as Norway, Sweden and Greece. The above interpretation can be justified by later developments. For example, Mr. Thorn, in his statement to the Parliament on 19 November 1980, urged the Parliament to appreciate the member states' realistic policy towards Turkey. He also indicated that the "foreign ministers were trying to exert pressure on the Turkish military leaders as they did in the Council of Europe." (44) The statement was a clear indication that the Council and the member states were trying to put pressure on Turkey, but in a discreet manner behind closed doors and outside the formal platforms of the Community.

The official contacts and meetings between the EC and Turkish officials and politicians that took place in the first year of the military regime supports the above claim. For example, when a delegation of the Commission met with Turkish diplomats in November 1980, to discuss emergency aid of 75 million ECU to Turkey, the issues of human rights and democracy were not raised. (45) The EC-Turkey Association Council also met in December 1980 at ambassadorial level. After the meeting, the Association Council reaffirmed the Community's intention that existing legal, political and economic ties should be maintained and negotiations for the preparation of the Fourth Financial Protocol should be carried out. (46) Again, in December of the same year when the Turkish officials met their counterparts to discuss visa requirements by the Benelux countries, France and Germany, the issues of human rights and democracy were not on the agenda. (47) Furthermore, Turkey was invited for consultations with the EPC mechanism "in order to assuage Turkey's concerns related to the accession of Greece to the Community as a full member in 1981." (48) In summary, with the exception of cancellation of the JPC meeting scheduled for 21 – 24 October 1980, all business between the Community and Turkey was carried out as normal. Since the Turkish Parliament (Turkish Grand National Assembly-TNGA) was dissolved by the military coup, there was no practical or institutional base for the JPC meeting, so the cancellation of the meeting was not a part of critical policy but was a necessity.

While the low profile policy of the EC towards Turkey was mainly a result of security and strategic considerations it had two basic problems. One, it was wrongly assumed that the military regime would be forced to restore democracy as a result of incentives implied by the Community's soft approach. Secondly, it neglected the likely implications of such an approach for the quality of the democratization process that Turkey might embark upon. In fact, there was near consensus among the top politicians of Europe that the Junta would eventually restore the democratic regime. They thought and gave indications that the military regime would be aware of the importance of the EC for Turkey's economic and political ties with the West. However, being aware of the permissive approach of the EC, the Turkish military Junta carried out its harsh policies freely and began to signal highly worrying intentions about the timetable as well as the nature of the democratization programme. After the first initial stages of establishing itself both domestically and externally, the Junta avoided giving a clear time - table for the restoration of democratic institutions and refrained from any commitment about the quality of the democratization that it had in mind. Furthermore, on many occasions, Kenan Evren, the head of the Junta, asked the Europeans not to interfere in Turkey's internal matters.

As the human rights violations increased, the military regime showed no intention of restoring democracy. On the other side, the European Parliament moved towards a tougher stand against the military regime. One such tough warning came in April 1981 with the adoption of a parliamentary resolution. In the plenary meeting of 10 - 11 April 1981 the Parliament adopted a resolution that, "called on the Commission, the Council and the member states to take up their responsibilities". It also requested Ankara to present a definite list of measures for the protection of human rights. Furthermore the resolution asked the Community and its member states to notify Turkey that "the association agreement would be immediately suspended if Turkey did not return to democracy within two months". (49) This resolution was the first critical resolution in Turkish-Community relations after the military takeover that put the association agreement in question. The Turkish military regime was confused in its reaction, " on the one hand, they tried to play the resolution down as a powerless decision without any implication, on the other they strongly condemned it as an unlawful interference in Turkey's domestic affairs."(50) In relation to the issue, Evren stated that "the Europeans cannot intimidate us with such a decision" (51) and blame the European leftist and the Socialists for engineering the resolution. Greece was also blamed for its support of the resolution on the grounds that "it was carried out by the Socialist - Greek front against Turkey". (52) However, the resolution had an immediate implication on the EC-Turkey relations. As a direct result of the Parliamentary pressure the Commission had to accept the parliamentary plan to send the parliamentary mission to investigate human rights violations in Turkey. (53)

However, just a month after the row that was sparked by the resolution of the Parliament over democracy and human rights in Turkey, "the Association Council agreed on the draft of the Fourth EEC - Turkey Financial Protocol."(54) It was obvious that despite the Parliament's resolutions and the pressure on the Commission and the Council, relations between Turkey and the Community were improving at Executive level. This encouraged the military regime even to spell out their desire for full membership. In an association meeting in June 1981, the Turkish ambassador expressed his Government's decision to speed up and intensify preparations at home so that Turkey could apply for full membership as soon as parliamentary democracy was restored. (55) This issue was indeed discussed in a Cabinet meeting following the accession of Greece in January 1981 and the Turkish government decided to apply for full membership after the restoration of democracy and the return to civil rule. This was a clear indication that the military rulers were aware that integration into the European Community required the establishment of a fully democratic political system. It was also a sign that, despite the public rows between the Community, particularly the Parliament, and the military rulers, behind closed doors they understood each other. Perhaps that was why the relations between Turkey and the EC were to a large extent uninterrupted in the early years of the military regime.

In mid June 1981, the Fourth Protocol was completed. The Protocol provided grants and loans amounting to 600 million ECU. This was an even better deal for Turkey when compared to the Third Protocol, which was signed during civilian rule. "The new protocol increased the EC's aid to Turkey by about 94 per cent over previous ones". (56) What was even more interesting was that the agreement was concluded just after the two months given to Turkey by the EP to restore democracy or face suspension of the association agreement.

This move, as expected, provoked anger in the EP and created tension between the EP and the Commission. The Commission and the Council were criticized for their actions towards Turkey. The Parliament also signaled that it would block the release of part of the emergency aid through the decision of its committee on budgets. (57) The Parliament's action to block the emergency aid eventually paid off. The Commission, in an attempt to avoid such an outcome, proposed to the Council on 7 December 1981 that the funds should be paid through the European Investment Bank (EIB) where Parliament approval was not required. However, the Council did not accept the proposal and suspended the approval of the emergency aid and made the release conditional on the improvement of the human rights situation and return to democracy in December 1981. (58) Nevertheless, this was not only due to the Parliament's pressure, but also because such an action would be resisted by some member states particularly Greece, Denmark, Luxemburg and France. The evidence indicates that the Council decision to block the emergency aid was closely related to an EP warning given to the Council in November 1981. (59) Nevertheless, making the release of emergency and other economic aid conditional on developments in the internal politics of Turkey was a policy, which sought to use economic pressure on the military regime in the hope of a rapid return to democracy and respect for human rights. This was "a stick disguised as a carrot", which remained as a policy instrument for the Community throughout the period. However, this policy did not work. In the view of the Parliament and some member states, Turkey was not moving towards the restoration of democracy as it had promised. The Council, on the other hand, "was more sympathetic to Turkey and on many occasions expressed its trust in the military leaders to restore democracy". (60) In fact, the end of the year 1981 was marked with signs of tension and irritation between the policy - making bodies of the EC on one hand and the member states on the other. The differences between the member states also became apparent over relations between Turkey and the EC. While small member states such as Denmark, Greece and the Netherlands, which were later joined by France, took a line close to that of the EP and tried to take a more critical stance, some larger states, such as Germany and Britain, maintained their support for the military regime.

However, at the end of 1981 the relations of the two parties moved into crisis due to the continuing harsh policies of the military regime. Despite the Junta's early promises, there were no concrete steps taken by the NSC in the direction of restoring democracy except the appointment of a consultative assembly in October 1981. However, even this first move to restore civil rule was over-shadowed by a NSC decree abolishing all the political parties, which existed prior to the military takeover on 12 September 1980. (61) Turkey's relations with the Community deteriorated even fur-ther when the former Prime Minister, Bulent Ecevit, was impris-oned for four months for breaching a NSC decree banning all po-litical statements.

These two decisions caused the pro-Turkey groups and cir-cles in the Community great difficulties in facing anti-Turkish lob-byists. This time, the Community moved quickly and strongly con-demned the dissolution of political parties and the imprisonment of Mr. Ecevit. Both cases were described as setbacks to the process of restoring democracy. This process, which the Community regarded as central to its relations with Turkey, was not seen to be improv-ing at all. A day after Ecevit's conviction, the Turkish ambassador to the EC was called in to convey the Community's message that the sentence raised doubts about a speedy return to democracy. (62) Following these developments the Commission concluded that, " under these circumstances it would not resume the decision of the release of the Fourth Financial Protocol." (63) The Turkish Gov-ernment's attempts to ease the tension and stop the process proved ineffective.

Finally, in December the Commission issued a statement in which, after mentioning the imprisonment of Ecevit, it was made clear that the Commission would not recommend a conclusion by the Council of the Fourth EEC - Turkey Financial Protocol which had been ready for signature since June. (64) This statement was issued a day after Ecevit was put in jail to serve his sentence. Per-haps the Commission was starting to have doubts about the assur-ances given by the NSC about the restoration of democracy. The Commission's statement that suspended the implementation of the

Fourth Protocol also came a week after the dissolution of political parties in Turkey. (65) The primary reason for the Commission's hard attitude in its strong declarations against Turkey was that the dissolution of the political parties and imprisonment of Evecit were seen as serious setbacks to the process of re-democratization. The second and less important reason was that, after the dissolution of political parties, some leading Turkish politicians, in contrast to their initial silence, "started to lobby against the military regime and asked their European contacts to increase pressure on the generals about the fate of democracy."(66)

The Commission's decision to stop the implementation of the Fourth Protocol and the Council's previous decision stopping the release of the emergency aid were serious blows for the Turkish economy at a time when the government was so much in need of foreign aid to implement its economic programme. With the above economic sanctions and signals of more to come Turkey was beginning to feel the pain. It was also aware that the Commission and the Council were now closer to the Parliament's stand than ever before. So the Turkish government decided to send its Foreign Minister to Brussels to talk to the Commission and explain the Turkish position. When the Minister visited the Commission in 1982, he tried to assure it that Turkey was preparing for civil rule and stated that the drafting of the new constitution had already begun. At the same time a timetable for a return to civil rule had been announced. He also passed on the news that Evecit was soon to be released from prison. (67) However, the Foreign Minister's attempt was ineffective in changing the negative attitude of the Community and the Minister was warned by the Commissioner about the ongoing trial of trade union leaders of the Revolutionary Workers Unions Confederation (DISK). He was also warned that the trial of the trade union leaders was subject to a resolution in the Parliament.

In its resolution of 22 January 1982, the Parliament condemned the trial and urged Turkey to respect basic human rights. In the same resolution the Parliament invalidated the mandate of its delegation to the JPC. (68) When the Parliament took this decision it was thought and interpreted both in European and Turkish circles as an insignificant move. The general interpretation of the decision, in Turkey, was that since the Turkish Parliament had already been dissolved, the EP's decision, in practice, did not make much difference in the relations between the EC and Turkey. However, later developments proved the contrary. First of all, the dissolution of the JPC delegation had the implication of rendering the work of the Association Council incomplete. Secondly, it was vitally important in its future implications because the European Parliament declined to renew the mandate even after the 1983 general elections. This both in practice and theory meant that the EP did not recognize the legitimacy of the new Turkish Parliament, which was elected for the period 1983-1987. The EP renewed its mandate only in September 1988. While Turkey was moving towards the return to civil rule by preparing a new constitution and electoral law, the Community as a whole seemed to take a more critical stance and initiated an active high-profile human rights policy in its relations with Turkey. In a sense, the Commission, the Council and, with the exception of Germany, the member states had become closer to the parliament's stance.

To keep the pressure mounting, the Council of Foreign Ministers sent its first strong message to Turkey in January 1982. The President of the Council, the Belgian Foreign Minister, Mr. Tindemans, told the Turkish Foreign Minister that "in view of prevailing opinions among the member-states, Turkey must fulfil various conditions if it wanted to maintain its association with the Community."(69) In February 1982, the Council of Foreign Ministers declared its decision to send a Presidency Mission to Turkey to discuss human right issues and the political situation in the country and express their expectations for an early return to democracy. (70) The visit took place on 19 March 1982 and, on behalf of the Community, Mr. Tindemans firmly told the authorities what was expected from Turkey and expressed deep concern about human rights conditions in the country. He particularly raised the issues of a rapid return to democracy, the release of political prisoners and trade unionists. He also demanded the end of martial law. (71) When he met Kenan Evren Tindemans was assured that the country was soon to return democracy. (72) On his return from Turkey, Mr. Tindemans reported to the Council and the Council issued a communiqué on 30 March 1982. The communiqué stated that "human rights violations in Turkey were of considerable concern and stressed that the country should be returned to democracy as soon as possible."(73) The European Council somehow believed that Mr. Tindemans' visit to Turkey contributed to the achievement of the Council's objectives in Turkey to accelerate the return of democracy. (74)

In the summer of 1982, political tension between Turkey and the Community rose again on the issue of Ecevit's second conviction. The Commission "condemned the new sentence on Ecevit as yet another setback to the process of restoring democracy". (75) Following the new development, an earlier report was debated and approved by the political committee in which the military regime was urged to give a precise timetable for a return to democracy. The French delegation "inserted a call on the Turkish government to grant cultural rights to the Kurdish and Armenian people."(76) 1982 also witnessed an unprecedented move by some member states, which was the biggest blow to the EC - Turkey relations. France, Denmark and the Netherlands together with two other non - EC member states (Norway and Sweden) made their complaint against Turkey at the ECHR on 2 July 1982. Turkey was accused of a violation of various human rights principles of the Council of Europe. (77) Despite Turkey's assurances of an early return to democracy and its preparation for a referendum for the new constitution, the Community as a whole began to take a relatively critical stance against human rights violations in the country, and implemented a high-profile active human-rights policy in its relations with Turkey.

There were five basic reasons for this. First, the Community eventually realized that it could use the economic means, particularly aid packages, and political means to affect the democratization situation in Turkey. The Community also hoped to accelerate the timing for the return to democracy and influence the democratization process. Second there was almost a consensus among the member states that the military leadership was not taking proper and sufficient steps to restore democracy and would not do so unless it was isolated and the pressure was increased. The member states began to feel that the permissive policy that had been introduced in the first year of the military regime was no longer a valid and appropriate framework for pursuing their strategy. Third the Parliament started to regard the situation in Turkey as a test case for its assertive human rights policy. Also, many MEPs had difficulties in justifying the EC's soft approach towards Turkey while it was taking a more active and critical stance against Poland in a high-profile policy. Fourth the Community itself was under pressure from European public opinion. This was partly attributed to those who had to leave Turkey after the military coup and sought refuge in European countries where they began lobbying against Turkey and forming a front with their European counterparts. In addition European trade unions and NGOs, Press Associations, Amnesty International, Helsinki Watch and other organizations, with firm support by some political parties, were pressing the Community to take a firm stand against the prolongation of the military regime in Turkey. (78) Fifth, there was the Greek factor, for the Greek accession into the Community with a Greek presence in both the Council and the Parliament had important negative effects on the overall relations between the EC and Turkey.

The military Junta had already been in power for more than two years and had reached the point when it could not postpone the holding of elections for much longer. While the new constitution was about to be put to a referendum and a date to be announced for the next general elections, the Europeans tended to give some time to Turkey to carry out the reforms. On the other hand, "Turkey was trying very hard with high level visits to the Commission to cool political tension and solve the economic problems."(79) In 1983, despite strong criticism over the new electoral law that gave approval power to the NSC on the participating political parties and individual candidates and over some provisions of the new constitution that were regarded as undemocratic, the Community seemed to adopt, once again, a wait-and-see-policy. It was obvious that it was prepared to give time and space to the military regime until the general elections took place. The Turkish government took advantage of the easing of tension between itself and the Community, and requested the Community to review its position on the Fourth Protocol. This was turned down on the basis that a decision would be taken at a later date. (80)

Nevertheless it was difficult to incorporate the European Parliament in the above process. Despite the obvious step towards the return to civilian rule, the Parliament did not compromise its stance. It adopted a new resolution three weeks before the general elections, on 13 October 1983. The resolution stated that the "so-called democratization process was a farce and the rules under which the elections were to be held prevented them from being a true expression of democracy". (81) For Turkey, the strong criticism of the Parliament and its displeasure about the whole democratization process was a result of " lack of understanding of the nature of Turkey's problems." (82) This was also attributed to the combination of liberals, leftists and Greek hostility against Turkey in the Parliament.

Finally general elections were held in November 1983. The Motherland Party won the election and a civilian government was formed under the leadership of the former deputy Prime Minister of the military regime, Tugut Ozal. After the election Turkey hoped to improve its image and relations with the community. However, the developments proved the opposite. Despite civil rule and the Turkish Government's efforts for a normalization of relations, there were clear indications that the Community, especially the Parliament, would keep pressing for full-scale democratization in Turkey. In the coming years, therefore, the relations between the EC and Turkey were dominated by the issues of human rights and democratic reforms.

7) The Second Phase: The civilian government and the EC 1983 - 1990

When a civilian government came to power after the November 1983 general elections, it was widely believed that the overall relations with Europe would be improved. In this context, Turkey solely concentrated on the normalization of its relations with two main components of Europe: The European Community and the Council of Europe. While the latter meant credentials and a prestige platform where Turkey's Europeanness could be approved, membership of the EC was the ultimate aim of Turkey's Westernisation program.

This was clearly set out in the first post-military regime civilian Government's program. The first Ozal government, in its programme, stated "the membership of the Community as its ultimate aim". (83) As a pragmatic economist, Ozal truly believed that Turkey's relations and co-operation with Western Europe should not be exclusively centered around a common defence strategy. In his view, closer economic ties were essential in order to integrate Turkey structurally into Europe and he believed that these ties would make Turkey an indispensable part of Europe. (84) Furthermore, Ozal and other leading politicians, as well as the military elites, hoped that the formal return to civilian rule would enable Turkey to regain its seat among the democratic Western European countries. The Ozal government was also expecting the re-activation of the association agreement and the release of the financial aid which were both suspended after the 1980 military coup. However, as will be illustrated, the opposite proved to be the case.

As far as the EC was concerned, there were two main obstacles in the way of the normalization of relations with Turkey. First, the pre-1983 general election political developments and the nature of the process of democratization, which was summarized in a EP resolution adopted on 13 October 1983 as "....a farce and the rules under which the elections were held prevented them from being a true expressions of democracy." (85) Second, despite the formation of a civilian government, the continuation of martial law, the political restrictions on the former politicians, regulations on the press and trade unions, and the ongoing mass trials of the DISK and members of the Peace Association as well as large number of intellectuals and journalists, were seen as an extension and a continuation of the military regime. As a result of this, Turkey's de facto frozen relations with the EC in the first years of the Ozal government did not start to move. Instead, unlike the Council of Europe, the EC, particularly the EP, continued to make the normalization of its relations conditional on improvements in Turkey's human rights record. The prevailing view was that, despite the general elections and the fact that the present situation was slightly better than before, Turkey was still a far cry away from being a free democracy. Many European politicians, particularly Socialists and Social Democrats, were therefore sceptical about the possibility of a democratic polity based on the 1982 constitution that, in their view, contained many illiberal and undemocratic articles. (86)

Shortly after the formation of Ozal's first government, Turkey started lobbying against the above perception. In January 1984, the Turkish Foreign Secretary, Vahit Halefoglu, paid a visit to Brussels. During the formal discussions between the Commission and the Secretary on the possibility of reviewing the Association Agreement, he was informed that the EC would only examine the question of reviewing EC-Turkey relations in the light of further developments concerning the "restoration of democracy and respect for human rights". (87)

The Commission's stance, however, was not shared by all the member states. In fact, the Commission's decision was the result of a lack of consensus in the Community rather than of a solid policy. In brief, the pre-election political developments and Turkey's human rights record had initially had a negative effect on the basis of the Community's human rights policy towards Turkey. The member states fell into two main blocks. While the member states, which took action against Turkey in the Council of Europe, maintained their uncompromising position until the end of 1984, the British and German governments started to show more open support for Turkey. (88) Both governments declared that they were not against Turkey's assumption of the Council of Europe Presidency on 22 November 1984. (89) Turkey has always seen the post as a ratification of its European credentials. It is a prestigious post, which Turkey had to give up in May 1981 as a direct result of the military coup. The German and British governments also gave their support to Turkey within the EC and wanted to ease the relations with Ankara. However, the German and British support for Turkey did not have much effect on the other member states. The divergence between the member states became even more obvious in the Dublin meeting of Foreign Ministers in September 1984. Although the ministers discussed the question of Turkey, they failed to reach a decision on the issue. (90) The situation created a dilemma as well as a clear divergence in the Community's governing bodies. As Ugur puts it "the Community was still critical of Turkey's human rights records but it was not able to update its stance in the light of the new developments in Turkey." (91) In fact, while Turkey was altering its stance and demanding a normalization of its relations, the Community lacked a consensus on the way in which it should deal with Turkey. While the parliament kept its original strong, critical position, which was clearly stated in its early resolution, the Council and some member states started openly to show more support for Turkey.

This view was clearly indicated and made public by the Italian presidency in April 1985. It was also conveyed to the parliament by Mr. Andreotti, who said, the way forward for the community was to build on recent improvements and encourage further achievements. (92) This not only indicated the differences between the Council and the Parliament, but also created a question of how effective such a policy would be in view of the half-hearted democratization process. This was also the most significant factor that contributed to the Community's dilemma in its policy towards Turkey. The dilemma was: should the EC agree to new initiatives aimed at accelerating the process of democratization or should it stick to its fundamental policy of wait - and - see. These two different - in fact opposite - stances were favoured by different bodies in the Community. This divergence continued to have a negative effect on the Community's policy towards Turkey in the following years. The later developments also indicated the growing independence of the Parliament from the Commission, the Council and member states, regarding the issues of human rights and democracy in Turkey-EC relations. The Parliament emerged as a significant platform, which looked to be able to influence the relations between the Community and Turkey and impose conditions on Turkey before a normalization of relations. Two main factors played a role in this development. First, after the re-admission of the Turkish delegation to the Parliamentary Assembly of the Council of Europe (PACE) which marked the normalization of political relations with Turkey, the Community was left as the only European major political and economic power able to influence the human rights policy in Turkey. Yet the divergence between the main governing bodies of the Community and the lack of consensus between the member states on whether it should be the "carrot or stick policy", towards Turkey raised the importance of the Parliament. Second, Ankara's desire to normalize its relations with the Community and re-activate the Association Agreement enabled Parliament to underline its conviction that "respect for human rights is one of the cornerstones of European co-operation ...and an important element in the relations between the third countries and the Community". (93) It can be argued that, in the absence of a consensus among the member states and the lack of a strong policy by the Council, the Parliament took the opportunity to employ the Community's formal policy, which was stated as "the Community in its relations with non-member states and in the administration of aid the promotion of human rights will be taking into consideration". In other words, the employment of diplomatic, political and economic means was regarded as justified to promote respect for human rights. The resolution also noted that "...expression of concern at violations such rights cannot be considered interference in the domestic affairs of a state." (94) In practice, the Community at large, as a result of the Parliament's determination and initiatives, went beyond the public denunciation of Turkey's human rights record and the lack of democracy and employed pressures through economic, political and diplomatic channels.

However, at the same time, the differences between the Parliament and some of the member states became greater than ever. While the Parliament and, to some extent, the Commission were becoming more critical of Turkey, the Council and some member states became more supportive of the new Turkish regime. The Belgian and British governments had moved further towards the German stance, and were in favour of lifting the ban on financial aid to Turkey. The British government made this public in the Foreign Secretary's speech on 13 February 1985 in which he suggested that the ban on financial aid to Turkey should be lifted.

However, as a lack of consensus on the issue still existed, the Council did not discuss, at least formally, the suggestion. Instead the relevant committees discussed the matter "... with a view to secure an agreement in the light of the developments in Turkey". (95) In 1985 the other member states, which were known as hardliners, also softened their position towards Turkey. France, Denmark and the Netherlands started to explore the possibility of reaching a friendly settlement with Turkey, under the brokerage of the Council of Europe Human Rights Commission. Turkey received a suggestion for a settlement from the above governments on 22 February 1985. The Ozal government acted swiftly and responded on 4 March 1985, which opened a direct channel of communication between the two parties. Finally, in December 1985, Turkey agreed "to strictly observe its obligations implied by article 3 of the ECHR and report to the Commission regularly in 1986."(96) Germany, as the biggest partner to Turkey in Europe and its greatest ally at the time, played its part effectively in order to normalize relations. The German Chancellor, Helmut Kohl, visited Turkey on 10 July 1985. This was the first visit of a head of a European government to Turkey after the military coup. The two days visit got tremendous publicity. Belgium also joined the race by offering Turkey a generous loan of BF250 million on 15 July 1985 shortly after Chancellor Kohl visit Turkey. (97)

As many commentators rightly pointed out, beside Turkey's strategic importance, the willingness of the member states to normalize relations with Turkey was not because of Turkey's return to democracy but mainly a result of the race between the member states to get a bigger share in the lucrative trade and investment opportunities created by Ozal's liberal economic policies. The country's high growth rates, rapidly increasing foreign trade and large military expenditure at the time made Turkey the center of attraction for European companies. When the situation was publicized in the press, the governments of the member states faced some difficulties in justifying their overtures towards Turkey. They had to try to neutralize domestic pressure by pointing to the progress made by Turkey in the field of human rights and democratization. Ironically the Turkish public was reading the same sort of reports in the Turkish media. For example, the daily newspaper, Hurriyet, in its front page reported that the award of the second Bosphorous Bridge to the Japanese was closely related to Turkey's annoyance with the Europeans. (98) Another leading paper (Milliyet) stated that the friendly settlement was the result of a failure on the part of the investors from applicant countries to get their share in Turkish investment projects that was estimated at over 3 billion US dollars in 1985 alone. (99)

However, despite the member states' efforts to improve their relations at a Community level, relations with Turkey were not improving. Furthermore, in1985 Turkey's relations with the Community faced a huge setback. Two important developments contributed to this. First, the controversial Balfe reports of the Political Affairs Committee, arrived at the conclusion that "Turkey's human-rights practice was still far from complying with the most elementary standards and recommended a further suspension of the setting up of the Joint Parliamentary Committee (JPC)."(100) This report was accompanied by the Parliament resolution of 23 October 1985, which condemned the practice of torture, death sentences, restrictions on foreign politicians and trade unions, continuing mass trials, and the repression of the Kurdish minority. More importantly, in this resolution the EP put five specific conditions for restoring its relations with Turkey: "The abolition of the death penalty, putting an end to torture and prosecution of all tortures, ending mass trails, granting the individual right of petition to the

ECHR and removal of all restrictions on the freedom of opinion".
(101) This resolution was in practice the most important of all those
to date. It contributed a significant new step in the parliament's
policy towards human rights and democracy for three reasons.

First, it marked the determination of the EP to block the
normalization of relations with Turkey despite the member states'
efforts to improve them. Second, it reflected the growing independence of the EP from the national governments of the member
states as well as from the Council. Third, and most importantly, it
was the first document that moved from general references to democracy, liberties, human rights and opened a new strategy in its
relations with Turkey by pointing out specific policy issues as the
minimum conditions for the establishment of normal relations. The
resolution was also important in its timing, because it coincided
with the growing desire of the Turkish government to improve its
relations with the Community speedily and at a time when Turkey
was enjoying relatively good relations with the member states.
Therefore it was regarded as a major setback to the normalization
of Turkey's relations with the Community.

As was to be expected, the resolution and the report created
tremendous anger and an almost hysterical reaction in Turkey. The
paper was perceived as a dangerous document that aimed to stop
the positive steps of the member states towards a normalization of
relations and the re-activation of the association agreement. The
Turkish Foreign Office described the resolution as "based on a pre-
conceived idea and stated that it dealt a blow to the prestige and
credibility of the Parliament in Turkey."(102) Furthermore, the
Community's representative was publicly accused of misinforming
the rapporteur of the Community. (103) Some politicians placed the
blame on Greek and socialist members of the Parliament. The
Turkish Prime Minister Ozal even crossed diplomatic language
boundaries and told the press that the rapporteur of the Parliament,

Richard Balfe, "was a crook and Turkey did not need the EC aid of 600 million ECU."(104) The second development that contributed to the set back in the EC-Turkey relations was a diplomatic one and concerned the Commission. Mr. Owen Morgan, the Commission representative in Turkey, made a public statement in June 1985 in which he commented that Turkey's relations with the Community would be set back for a decade if the Turkish Parliament (TNGA) enacted the draft bill granting new powers to the police force. (105) The Turkish government reacted angrily and made it clear that Mr.Morgan's public statement and interference in Turkey's domestic affairs was not acceptable and was not suitable for a diplomatic mission. After mounting criticism, the Commission had to withdraw Mr. Morgan on safety grounds. (106) However, Mr. Morgan soon resumed his post in Ankara with the full support of the Commission. This incident both reflected and contributed to the development of a hard line policy on the part of the Commission.

Despite some positive political developments in Turkey, 1986 was also a year of struggle in the normalization of EC Turkish relations. The differences and divergences between the Council and member states on one hand and the Parliament, later joined by the Commission, on the other, increased in this year. I believe that this was mainly due to the Community's internal developments and Turkey's new initiative to adopt legal and political measures in order to improve its human rights records. In 1986, the Community's over-all human rights activities were intensified. This year the Single European Act was adopted referring specifically to the human rights dimension in the European Community's external relations. (107) The EPC also issued a comprehensive statement that made respect for human rights an important element in its relations with third countries. Thus member states' attempts to normalize relations with Turkey at a time when a high-profile human rights policy was beginning to emerge were bound to be problematic. This proved to be correct by the end of the 1986 when the Parliament took action against Turkey.

The same developments also showed that the Parliament could complicate the task of the member states and the Council as well as the Commission by maintaining its critical stance against Turkey. The parliament's uncompromising stance was also encouraged by Turkey's eagerness to normalize its relations with the Community. In fact, being aware of the Community's stance and the divergence within the Community, Turkey tried to soften the Parliament's approach by adopting some legal and political measures. However, internal factors also started to influence the Turkish government regarding the reforms. Although the former political leaders were legally prohibited from politics or even expressing their opinion on political matters they began to play an active role in organizing opposition forces against the government in a discreet manner. The main extra-parliamentary opposition parties increased their activities towards human rights issues and legislative changes mainly in relation to lifting the political ban on the former political leaders. This undoubtedly boosted the internal demand for human rights and democratization in the country. As a result, of this political activities and public demands for reforms and democratization by opposition parties, and non-governmental organizations increased. Hunger strikes were also started by the prisoners and their supporters in protest against prison conditions in the country. The military establishment and the conservative elite have always claimed that the internal demand for democratization was a part of an outside conspiracy aimed to sabotage Turkey's relations with Europe. (108) Although, this claim does not hold much water, there was certainly foreign support for and involvement in the internal demand for democratization and on improvement of human rights in the country. This also led to more open debates on the political system and particularly on human rights issues. Trade unions, the press, human rights organizations (all of which were established after the military regime) and the private sector also joined the debate and started to demand more freedom and a change in the undemocratic articles of the constitution and related laws. The opposition forces often based their arguments on the need for Turkey to reform its political system and lift the undemocratic features of the 1982 constitution in order to improve its relations with the EC. They also emphasized that the government should do so not simply to please Europe but for its own citizens. They thus argued that European demands coincided with the needs of the country. (109)

Although the military and conservative forces used the democratization reforms as a tactic to gain European support and as strategic moves towards membership of the EC, some segments of Turkish society (i.e. the private sector particularly financial sector, trade unions and civil organizations) genuinely believed in reforms. However, aware of their limited capacity in influencing the conservative forces and military establishment they did not hesitate to use the EC and other European organizations as additional elements to bring about the reforms. On the other hand, some segments of the society, for example, Kurdish, Islamists and leftists often tried to use the EC as an external agent to support their causes with regard to legal and democratic reforms in spite of their distrust to the Europeans. (110)

The government, in order to improve its image in Europe and respond to internal demands lifted the ban on public speeches by former politicians. A partial amnesty was also declared, leading to the release of 31,000 prisoners including the detainees of DISK and Peace Association. (111) These developments were recognized in various European international organizations. The ECHR dropped the case against Turkey by agreeing a friendly settlement. Turkey began to chair the OECD and was offered the presidency of the Council of Europe in the same year. These were signs of the improving image of Turkey in European political institutions. This of course led the Turkish government to hope for a similar turn in the relations between Turkey and the EC. In fact, the Community was taking note of the normalization in Turkey's relations with other European political organizations, in some of which the member states were dominant.

Therefore, the Turkish government, perhaps after being encouraged by some member states, expressed its wish to activate the EC - Turkey Association Council at Ministerial level. The Turkish call for the Council meeting was received by the Foreign Ministers in early 1986. (112) However, Turkey's enjoyment of this good news did not last long. The first strong reaction to the Council's intention came from the Parliament. 100 MEPs sent a letter to the Council, on 25 March 1986 to indicate their disagreement with those intentions. This letter did not change the Council's decision, but it prompted the Presidency to assure the MEPs that their concerns had been taken into account by the Council. (113) In fact, it forced the British Presidency to explain the situation to the MEPs. When asked for clarification, the British presidency through Sir Geoffrey Howe, told the Parliament that the decision to normalize relations ".... reflected the progress that Turkey has made in restoring democracy and the wish of the Council to encourage further reform". (114) However, this positive approach of the Council did not satisfy either the Parliament or the Commission. While the disagreement between the EC institutions on how to respond to Turkey's request was still fresh, Mr. Claude Cheysson, the Commissioner in charge of Mediterranean policy, paid a visit to Turkey on 19-20 June 1986.

This was the first visit by a member of Commission since the military coup. Following his visit Mr. Cheysson, told the press that "... the European people did not consider that fundamental rights are respected in Turkey... and more progress is expected by everyone." (115) Cheysson, while in Turkey, held meetings with the authorities, including the President Kenan Evren, and raised three particular issues, which were presented as obstacles to the normalization of EC-Turkey relations. The issues were human rights and democratization in general, the issue of free movement of persons which, according to the Association Agreement, was due by the end of 1986, and the problems caused by a 1964 decree that froze the assets of the Greek minority who had emigrated from North Cyprus and from Turkey to Greece during the Cyprus crisis of 1963. (116)

Despite the disagreement of the Parliament with the Council, the Association Council met in September 1986. This was the first meeting of its kind since the1980 military coup but, as was expected, no specific decision was reached in the meeting. Statements from both sides were carefully written, underlining the human rights issues and the re-establishment of democracy with emphasis on the need for more progress. While the Community stressed that further progress was essential to re-activate the Association Agreement and bring about a normalization of relations, the Turkish side gave details on what had been undertaken and assured its European counterparts that Turkey shared European values and that the government was committed to further reforms. (117)

Although the meeting ended without any specific decision on the re-activation of the Association Agreements or the release of the 600 million ECU aid to Turkey, which the Ankara government had pressed for, the Turkish side still regarded the meeting as successful and interpreted it as the go ahead for the normalization process. Ankara's most optimistic approach was, in fact, backed up by the British Foreign Secretary and the President of the Council of Ministers, who remarked on the occasion that Turkey was given "the green light to resume political and economic relations with the Community". (118) Turkey was also awarded some aid through the

1986 budget of the Community, giving the impression that the EC was moving closer to collaboration with her. (119) The Council, however, tried to assure the Parliament that it did not dissociate itself from the concerns of the Parliament about the human-rights practices in Turkey. (120)

These limited improvements in EC - Turkish relations were soon overshadowed by the continuing critical attitude of the Parliament. At the end of 1986, the Parliament adopted a new resolution on relations between Turkey and the EC. In this, it not only expressed its criticism about the shortcomings of the regime in the political and human rights fields, but also urged Turkey to pursue "a good relationship and a neighbour policy towards Greece and contribute to the solution of the Cyprus problem". The Parliament also declared that the Community was not yet justified in fully normalizing its relations with Turkey. Furthermore, criticizing the Council, it noted that "... the meeting of the Association Council gave the false impression that the EC endorsed the political and human rights situation in Turkey". (121) The MEPs' determination in their critical stance against Turkey led the Parliament not to re-establish the JPC, which had been cancelled in 1981 as a result of the military coup. This in practice meant that the EP did not recognize the legitimacy of the new Turkish Parliament.

This highlights the differences between the Council and the Parliament's stance as well as the Parliament's determination to block any move towards normalization in the Community's relations with Turkey. In other words, although the Parliament became aware of its limitations in pushing the Council and the member states towards a more critical stance, it saw the opportunity that was provided by Turkey's eagerness to establish relations with the EC. This enabled the Parliament to become a central platform where Turkey's human rights records were scrutinized and this led to the issues of human rights and democracy being brought to the top of the EC - Turkey agenda.

In short, the Parliament perceived the situation as a significant opportunity to pressure Turkey in order to implement new democratic reforms and improve its human rights record. In doing this, the Parliament has always argued that it was following the Community's code, and that its criticism of Turkey is justified. Although the Council and the member states tried to distance themselves from the Parliament's stance, behind closed doors they have always tried to assure the Parliament that its concerns are being taken into consideration. The Parliament noted these assurances and agreed to the "... continuation of dialogue to settle differences between Turkey and the Community"(122) but, as mensioned above, it refused to normalize its own relations with Turkey. This not only proved that the Parliament can complicate the whole process of normalization relations with Turkey, but also sent a signal that its power granted by the single European Act should not be ignored by Turkey, the member states or the Council. This also naturally slowed down the whole process and, from time to time, caused set backs.

However, despite the lack of good relations with the EC and critical stance of the EP Ankara declared its intention to apply for full membership in 1987. In the same year (1986), a Ministry of State responsible for Community Affairs was created. The Ministry embarked on a heavy lobbying campaign in the Western European capitals. (123) As part of its strategy, the Turkish government adopted a number of legal and political measures. The timing for the application was also carefully considered before it was lodged. The Ozal government believed that the democratic credentials of the Turkish regime were strengthening in Europe, Turkey in fact held the Presidency of the Council of Europe when it made the application. Nevertheless, the Ozal government started new reforms in order to eliminate the parliamentary criticism and to satisfy the Commission about its improving human rights record. The government adopted three measures that were designed to soften the Community's approach to Turkey. First, it declared that the 1964 decree (mentioned above) would be repealed. This was done particularly to score some points against Greece, which was seen as one of the main obstacles in Turkey's relations with EC. Second, Turkish citizens were granted the right of individual petition to the ECHR for a period of three years. (124) Third, a parliamentary committee was established within the National Assembly to monitor developments in the field of human rights. This move was in fact a response to, and compliance with, the Commission's demand, which was made during Mr.Cheysson's visit to Turkey in June 1986.

In 1987 the Ozal government also indicated that it was pre-pared to introduce further reforms in due course to improve its human rights standards. Nevertheless, the application in practice was the beginning of a new era in Turkey - EC relations. Once Turkey made the application for full membership, the Turkish gov-ernment was bound to move further into the sphere of Community influence and become more vulnerable than ever to external pres-sures particularly on the issues of human rights and democracy. The application naturally increased European public interest in Turkey's internal affairs and political system, which led to a con-tinuing public scrutiny of Turkey's human rights record. The Community was now able to dictate its opinion more vigorously on Turkish politics and internal affairs. In fact, the application gave political and even legal procedural justification for "external EC interference". It was obvious that, despite his portrayal of Turkey as politically fit for membership, Ozal was aware that his government needed to improve the image of Turkey by taking decisive steps towards new reforms in the direction of democratization and re-spect for human rights. In fact, the evidence shows that the Ozal government was not only aware of this situation, but also engaged in discreet debates with Community officials regarding the country's human rights record and was taking measures to satisfy the Europeans. In a debate in the EP, the Council tried to assure the Parliament that the policy of discreet intervention was paying off. While Mr. Tindemans noted the establishment of the Parliamentary Committee within the TGNA to monitor developments in the field of human rights as a concrete achievement, the Dutch Presidency stated that the "...... Turkish government understands the importance that the Twelve attach to human right as a result of ongoing discreet diplomacy."(125) The Parliament was also informed that EPC interest in the Kurdish issue went back to 1986, but the deliberations were kept secret. (126) This shows that, despite the prevailing opinion that the Turkish government would not compromise on the sensitive Kurdish issue the question was subject to discussions between the Community and Turkey.

The EP, encouraged by the favorable opportunity provided by the Turkish application, stepped up its pressure by adopting a sensitive resolution on the 18 June 1987 just two months after Turkey's application. The resolution described the displacement of the Armenian people by the Ottoman Empire in 1915-1917 as genocide and further asserted that "the Armenian question and the question of minorities {Kurds} must be ratified within the framework of relations between Turkey and the Community. (127) The resolution also asked the Council to obtain an acknowledgement from Turkey to the effect that the Armenian people had been subjected to genocide. Not surprisingly, the resolution caused tremendous anger in Turkey. The Turkish government's reaction was also hostile. President Evren, after expressing his disappointment stated that, "...some of Turkey's allies were asking Turkey to give away territory to others and this was a request that even the Warsaw Pact countries had not dared to make". He also named the resolution as " plot to obstruct Turkey's entry the EC."(128) A day later, the ambassadors of the Twelve were summoned into the Foreign Ministry and informed of the reaction of the Turkish government which regarded the resolution as "aimed at sabotaging the relations between the EC and Turkey and they were issued with a warning about European support for separatism". (129) The press described the resolution as an outrageous one, the political parties and parliamentarians also joined the race to condemn the resolution and the EP itself. However, despite all the strong reactions, the Turkish government had come to realize that the EP was a significant actor in its relations with the EC and should not be overlooked.

The Turkish government, keeping this in mind, agreed to an EP delegation to monitor the forthcoming general elections in November 1987. It also asked the President of the Council, Mr. Tygesen, whether it was the right time for Turkey to seek closer contacts with the EP. At the same time, the Turkish government was forced to amend the electoral law that had been heavily criticized by the EP and Turkish opposition forces. The EP delegation observed the elections in November 1987 and was satisfied that voting in the election took place in a correct manner. However, it criticized the government for its "manipulation of local authority grants and failing to further democratize the electoral law."(130)

Turkish democracy and the country's human rights record were in the spotlight again when the returning exiled Communist leaders were arrested on their arrival in Turkey. The EP immediately took action and strongly condemned their arrest and demanded the immediate release of Mr. Sargin and Mr. Kutlu. As a direct result of this development, the EP decided to block the protocol upgrading the Association Agreement following the accession of Spain and Portugal. (131) It also noted that the release of the Communist leaders would contribute to the establishment of democracy in Turkey. The evidence indicates that the decision of the Communist leaders to return to Turkey was an attempt to legalize the Communist Party, which was prompted by Turkey's application for full membership of the EC. The timing and style of the return of the Communist leaders, who were accompanied by European politicians, parliamentarians, representatives of Amnesty International and European journalists, made it clear that the exiled leaders' aim was not to just to return to their country but also to increase European pressure on Turkey. This was, indeed, recognized by the Turkish President and Premier, Ozal, who argued that the return of the Communists leaders to Turkey aimed to sabotage Turkish relations with the EC by putting the country's democratic credentials in question. (132) In the same year the Parliament also blocked the release of some financial aid to Turkey. On the other hand, the Commission proposed to finance three projects in Turkey by releasing the special aid decided in 1980, but postponed due to the military regime. (133) Although the proposed aid was not significant in its amount, it was important in showing the Commission's interest in Turkey and the different stance between the Commission and the Parliament. In fact, as illustrated above, in this period the EP became the main obstacle to the normalization of relations with Turkey. This created wide spread scepticism in Turkey about the role of the EP in blocking the re-activation of relations. Birand for example, argues that member states used the EP as a shield to avoid criticism by Turkey. Ozal even went further by claiming that "some European countries which found some Turkish goods competitive in the market, had tried to hide behind political issues and block re-activation of the relations between the two sides". (134)

However, whatever the reason for the Parliament's stance, the Turkish government and intellectuals at large became aware that membership of the Community and Turkey's further liberalization, including legalization of the Communist Party, were closely linked to each other. (135) Furthermore, the Turkish government came to realize that Turkey needed to win the Parliament's support in order to realize its bid for accession. As expected, before the Commission announced its opinion on Turkey's application, both leaders were released from prison and reforms were carried out by the Turkish government to legalize the formation of a Communist Party in the country.

By 1988, the member states and the Commission had moved further towards the Parliament's critical stance. Turkey saw the move as a negative development and, to soften the Community's approach to its waiting application, Ankara began to introduce various new measures with potentially positive implications for human rights. The 1964 decree, which was put in question by the Commission in early 1986, was abolished on 5 February 1988, just two months before the planned Association Council meeting. The European Convention on the Prevention of Torture was also signed in Turkey in January 1988 and one month later Turkey became the first country to ratify the convention in its Parliament. This was in spite of its refusal to sign the convention just a few months earlier in November 1987. (136) Turkey also ratified the UN Convention on torture in the same year. Its rapid change of policy and quick move to ratify the above conventions was interpreted as a sign of Turkey's realization that "...she must improve her human-rights image as she tries to become a full member of the EC." (137)

Turkey's adoption of new measures to improve its image regarding human rights and democracy seemed to be paying off. In September 1988 the Parliament agreed to re-activate the JPC for the first time since the 1980 military coup. Despite this positive development later developments showed that the meetings in the JPC tended to be more problematic for Turkey. Ugur argues that the parliament's decision to re-activate the JPC was a carefully designed move for two reasons. First, he noted that "the decision could enable the EP to transform the JPC meetings into a platform where pressure on Turkey could be exerted directly". Secondly, its timing coincided with the revision in the stance of the Council and the member states, which became closer to the Parliament's stance and therefore, according to him, "enabled the Parliament to weaken Turkey's criticism of it as the hot bed of extremism". (138) The developments in the following years proved that the above conviction was correct. The JPC meetings, which normally take place 2-3 times a year, became a debating platform where Turkey's human rights record was scrutinized. The EP delegation constantly used the meetings to ask for improvements in specific areas related to human rights and democracy in the country. Responses from the Turkish delegation often had to be in the form of written answers in advance of the planned meetings, so that the EP delegation could discuss the matter before the JPC meeting, and adopt a common approach. In these meetings, the questions normally related to very specific issues and particular articles such as 312, 141, 142, and 163 of the Turkish penal code that prohibited the organization of Communist or religious parties and the commutation of the death penalty into life sentences. A general or partial Amnesty was also discussed in these meetings. (139)

The situation was becoming more and more irritating for Turkey. However, as its application was on the table, the government tried to please the MEPs as much as possible. After 1988 almost all the correspondence between the Community organs and the Turkish government related to human rights issues in one way or another. The Spanish Presidency for example, made four statements to the Parliament in the first half of 1989 in which all the human rights issues were raised, and the Parliament was given assurances that the Council was following the case closely. For example, Mr. Ordonez told the MEPs that "human right issues had always been dealt with during both bilateral and joint Community contacts with Turkey."(140) Two months later he also informed the Parliament that specific EPC representations were made to the Turkish government on more than one occasion about the penal code articles mentioned above. He assured the MEPs that "the Turkish government was fully aware of the Community's views on this matters". (141) Another statement was made on 11 April 1989. In his reply to a parliamentary question, the President of the Council informed the Parliament that Turkey gave assurances that "...the application of its penal code is in accordance with the international human rights standards". He also added that "the evolution of the Association depends on progress in the field of human rights". (142) Later the Spanish Foreign Minister told the Parliament that "....as Turkey wishes to become a member of the Community, I must point out that it is this very Parliament which has the last word about the decision". (143)

Although it might be said that these initiatives and statements were closely related to the member states interests in blocking Turkey's membership, they were also related to the domestic pressure on EC governments. In this period the Kurdish issue and the unrest, particularly in the South Eastern part of Turkey, increasingly came to the attention of the European public. Large numbers of Kurdish refugees and their high-profile activities promoted this and, as a result, the Kurdish question started to become a dominant issue in Turkey's international relations. For example, in response to public concern about Turkey's treatment of the Kurdish minority, a hundred members of the German Bundestag issued a declaration containing five demands. They called on the Turkish government "to meet the September 1985 conditions of the EC," and added a few new conditions concerning the acceptance of the Kurdish minority's existence in Turkey. (144) This move is interesting in showing the change of attitude in the Bundestag, which had indicated its willingness to lift the ban on German financial aid to Turkey as early as December 1981.

Under these conditions, the Commission Opinion on Turkey's request for accession to the Community was declared on 20 December 1989 and ratified by the Council on 5 February 1990.

8) The European Influence on Turkish Politics and Democratisation, 1980 - 1983: the Military Regime and the EC

As explained above, for the Turkish elites -civilian and military alike- isolation of Turkey with Europe has always been unbearable. Therefore, even the first military communiqué was designed to calm down a possible European reaction to the coup of 1980. Aiming to calm the Europeans the military coup emphasised that they came to power to stop a possible disintegration of the country and safeguard the weak democracy. The leader of the Coup stated that they would hand the power to a civilian government as soon as possible. (145)

However, the military regime in the period 1980-1983 faced an intense and continued pressure from European quarters particularly from the EC and the Council of Europe as well as from non-governmental organisations such as Amnesty International, other human rights organisations, European trade unions, press associations and of course individual countries. As a result of this intense pressure, the military regime became defensive in its foreign policy with Europe. From the outset the military junta needed to explain itself, and justify the military take-over. As a result of this, internal affairs became an issue in Turkey's relations with Europe, particularly with the EC. On the other hand, the generals always denied the fact that they bowed to European pressure.

However, despite the junta's public defiance of Europe, the readiness to discuss internal matters with the Europeans revealed the European influence on the generals and the true attitude of the military regime. Furthermore, the military rulers' sensitivity and vulnerability to the European criticism became more apparent during the transition period. Believing in Westernization and keeping the European factor in mind, the military regime felt obliged to explain itself and discussed internal matters with Europeans at all levels. The military aim in doing this was to explain the future prospects of democracy in the country and assure the West that the military regime was temporary. On the other side, Europeans saw the weakness of the regime and intensified the pressure they exerted. As a result, this carried Turkey's internal affairs into its external relations with Europe and its relations with Europe became dependent on the domestic political developments. As explained above, many resolutions of the EP and decisions of the Commission and the Council referred to Turkey's internal political developments as pre-conditions for a normalisation of relations. On the other hand, Turkey's high level responses to these pressures were prime examples of the European influence on Turkey returning to civil rule and democratisation. (146)

European pressure had economic and political dimensions that, from time to time, created short-lasting confrontation and mutual distrust between the two parties and led to isolation in Turkey's relations with Europe. To overcome its economic problems, Turkey turned to its military ally, the USA, particularly for military aid, and strengthened its economic ties with the Middle Eastern Countries. As a result, from 1980 to 1982 while Turkish exports to the EC dropped from 44.7 percent to 31.4 percent of total exports, the Islamic countries' share in Turkish exports rocketed from 22.5 percent to 48.2 percent (see appendix 8). (147) During this period, Turkish-American relations also improved. In fact, this period was "a golden age" in Turkish-US relations. The US gave full support to the military regime and bilateral problems, which occurred following the 1974 Cyprus military intervention, were quickly solved. However, neither the US nor the Middle East was substituted for Turkey's strong historical, political, economic and military links with Europe. Since the military shared the common aim of the Turkish elite that Turkey should be integrated into Europe once and for all, it felt that relations should not be allowed to deteriorate further. Thus, the military regime needed to reach some sort of compromise to avoid a total breakdown in its relations with the EC as well as with the Council of Europe. As a result of this common but discreet approach, the military rulers tended to understand the European criticism within the context of being a member of European organisations, which upholds democracy and human rights. As one of the ruling components of the country, who were historically committed to westernisation, the military leaders took European criticism very seriously. The evidence shows that the European factor had a great impact on the military regime not only in returning Turkey to civil rule but also in implementing policies during their stay in power. The military rulers in this period had always to add into their calculations the possible response from Europe before a policy was adopted. They felt obliged to think over the possible cost of their actions in terms of the damage that would be inflicted on diplomatic, economic and military relations.

For example, during the discussions in the NSC on the dissolution of the political parties, its members were concerned that such an action could jeopardise Turkey's remaining links with the European states and organisations, particularly the EC. According to Evren, however, "their determination to finish off the old politicians and the internal opposition centres to the military regime over-rode the external concern". (148) This might be taken as an evidence of the military determination and their resistance to external pressure, but it actually illustrates the sensitivity of the Generals to European criticism. Another example of such concern came to light, towards the end of the military regime, when the NSC closed down the Great Turkey Party-Buyuk Turkiye Partisi (GTP) and sent 16 former politicians to internal exile. The evidence reveals that the Generals were concerned about possible European reactions and discussed the possible action that might be taken against them by the Europeans. (149) Mainly because of the above incidents, some observers accept the importance of the European factor but argue that it was impossible to say that the Europeans forced the military regime to restore democratic institutions. While Pridham finds the European pressure on Turkey to be "decisive factor promoting a return to democracy," (150) Karaosmanoglu comes to conclusion that the European factor "must have exerted an increasing influence on the process of democratisation in Turkey". (151) Dodd, disagrees with the above convictions but states that European pressure "obliged the military regime to make its aims very clear". (152)

As a matter of fact, right from the beginning, the military Junta made clear that its aim was to restore democracy. The Europeans did not have much doubt about this aim and to some extent there was a consensus both at home and abroad that the military regime was a temporary administration and, sooner or later, the military would hand over power to the civilians. However, it was not known how harsh and how long this regime was going to be. I would argue that the European impact was very effective, in shaping the return to civilian rule. In fact Europe was the only effective external force that influenced the military rulers and the whole process of returning to civilian rule. This was due to two reasons: the military's historical commitment to the Westernization of the country and Turkey's strong political, economic and military linkages to the west accompanied by an ultimate aim of Turkey's integration to Europe, by joining the EC as a full member. These two reasons determined the position of the military. For the same reasons, the Generals became more sensitive and vulnerable to the European criticism. Furthermore, Turkey's membership in the western organisations and its desire to become member to the EC constituted an international setting which "imposed its own principles and aspirations upon the desires and designs of the Turkish military."(153) Turkey's economic and military dependency on the West was also an additional factor in returning to civilian rule. Therefore, the Turkish military was not only aware of the importance of Turkey's place in Europe and the inappropriateness of a military regime in the country but also of the catastrophic consequence of a permanent military regime. Thus, European influence on the military rulers was effective both in the return to civilian rule and in the implementation of some of its policies during the period in office. (154) Evidence clearly indicates that despite their public defiance the military rulers and their diplomats have always engaged in an endless effort to persuade the Europeans of Turkey's commitment to democracy and human rights. Thus, the issues of democracy and human rights inevitably occupied the centre of Turkish foreign policy, which proves the intense interactions between the two sides. Moreover, the military regime could not remove these issues from the agenda altogether, so it engaged in discussions of them, in almost all diplomatic encounters.

This fact is very well documented in Evren's Memoirs, which are generally accepted as an authoritative account of the 1980 military coup. In his memoirs, Evren refers to the European dimension of internal political situations for each year and gives detailed accounts of the discussions with the Europeans. (155) The military regime's diplomatic and political weight was put into efforts to persuade the European capitals that democracy would be restored in the near future and that the human rights situation in the country would improve. This might be seen as a gesture to the European capitals. However, the evidence proved that it was more than this. This approach put Turkey on the defensive in its relations with Europe and provided a backbone for European influence. The general mood among high ranking administration officials was that, the European modest concerns with democracy and human rights were legitimate and understandable. In the case of the EC, this was officially acknowledged by the Turkish Foreign Minister as he put it "as far as Turkey's membership in the European organisations was concerned the concerns of the Europeans were legitimate." (156)

However, as explained above, the military regime had publicly rejected external interference in its home affairs. Nevertheless, their discourse was apologetic and permissive. For the generals, the crisis in Turkey was a matter of survival. They felt that they had to save the country from disintegration and that they needed to preserve the Kemalist regime. According to them this justified sacrifices in the fields of democracy and human rights. In their discourse they blamed the European allies for not understanding the whole situation in the country and often showed great resentment towards them. According to the military, state security and the defence of the Kemalist principles would be the ultimate priority. In fact, the above approach was a natural outcome of the Republican "state security discourse", which was based on the protection of Kemalist principles, the fight against communist and separatist danger and against political Islam. In this classical discourse the rights of the state would prevail over the rights of the people. (157) Accordingly, the military regime, strongly rejected criticism from European quarters and often put the blame on the anti-Turkish centres, particularly European and Turkish Marxists, as the source of the anti-Turkish campaign in Europe. The distinction between those with the bad intentions and the misinformed Europeans had always been made public. Under the military regime, almost all the anti-military regime oppositions in Europe, including the European

Human Rights Commission, were branded as the work of people who wanted to separate Turkey from Europe. These statements not only implied that Turkey did not want to be separated from Europe but also that Turkey should put all its efforts in explaining itself to the European capitals and organisations.

While European human rights activists were accused of being Marxist, leftist and supporters of Kurdish separatists or being pawns of Greece, the policies of the Council of Europe and the EC were denounced as contradicting the principles of friendship, good relations and the rules of international relations. Therefore, "publicly the military rulers always declared that they would not bow to European pressure". (158) However, this did not match the actual practices of the military regime. For example, Evren repeatedly expressed his annoyance with the regular flow of foreign observers from government officials, politicians, diplomats, human rights activities, trade unions, press associations etc. by saying that "they come to inspect us" (159) However, he did not, or could not stop Europeans from inspecting Turkey. Furthermore, every single announcement or resolution from the European Continent was taken seriously and led to comments and statements from Head of State, Evren, or other officials, which one way or another, indicated their sensitivity and the European influence.

The military regime was aware of the international tension in East-West relations, the political turmoil in the region and of Turkey's strategic importance for the alliance. The military rulers, therefore, tried hard to play the security and co-operation card by underlining Turkey's strategic and military importance for Western interests in a highly unstable region. In the first year of the military regime, this argument was reinforced by western strategic considerations and, to a large extent, shaped the Europeans' initial soft reaction to the military coup. However, as time passed, the European soft and permissive approach was replaced by a critical stance.

Individual European states then also joined the EC or the Council of Europe in criticising Turkey. As the pressure mounted, the military regime came to recognise the necessity to adjust its foreign and domestic policies to the changing European environment. A timetable for the return to democracy was the main issue that created tension between the Europeans and the military regime. This issue, alongside alleged human rights abuses, was raised on many occasions by European politicians, reporters and delegations both in the European capitals, and during their visits to Turkey. To this end, the EC and the parliament in particular constantly asked for a timetable for the return to democracy and made this a pre-condition for all their relations with Turkey. On the other hand, the Council of Europe threatened Turkey with expulsion if it did not return to democracy soon. Under all these pressures the military rulers, in order to prevent further isolation in Europe, declared a timetable for the return to civil rule some two years before actual elections took place and furthermore, just one month before the assembly meeting where Turkey's expulsion was going to be discussed.

The evidence indicates that the NSC announced the timetable for the general elections, specifically to assure the Europeans about the generals' commitment to establish a parliamentary democracy and to ease the pressure. The timing of the announcement increases this probability. The announcement came two years before the elections took place, but one month after the dissolution of the political parties which created an outrage in the Community and other European organisations, and just one month before the Assembly meeting where Turkish expulsion was to be discussed. At this time, the military regime was experiencing the most difficult period in its relations with the Community as well as with the Council of Europe. The imprisonment of Ecevit and dissolution of the political parties created a common criticism for the first time since the military coup. The Council of Europe decided to hold a meeting to suspend all its economic aid programmes to Turkey. The announcement was also made just a week before the arrival of a delegation from the Council would determine whether Turkey would be allowed to return in the Council of Europe. At such a critical time, the announcement of an approximate date for the general elections should be regarded as a move to stop this rapid deterioration in Turkey's relations with Europe, and to ease the general tension between Ankara and the European capitals. However, the above announcement of the military junta did not ease the relations with Europe.

In October 1983 just one month before the general elections, the EP and the Parliamentary Assembly of the Council of Europe separately denounced the pre-election process and declared the elections to be undemocratic and unrepresentative. Furthermore, the Parliamentary Assembly decided to bar the new Turkish MP's from the sessions. The Generals were alarmed with this decision and held an emergency meeting the same month to discuss the possibility of a last minute expulsion from the Council of Europe. (160) The emergency meeting gave a true picture of the military regime's attitude towards Europe. The Turkish military rulers and their civilian partners could not even think of taking a step backward in the direction of westernization by cutting Turkey's ties with the European Community or the Council of Europe. Such a move, according them, "would put Turkey's 'Europeaness' in question in the minds of the Turks as well as the Europeans, enhance domestic anti-modernist political groups and weaken Turkey's other memberships in the West." (161) For the above reasons, the military regime's priority in foreign policy was to continue Turkey's membership of European organisations and avoid any major confrontation that might lead to the expulsion of Turkey or suspension of its relations. To avoid this, the regime more often reversed its decisions or changed policy.

For example, the military regime was strongly criticised by the EC and member-states over the long detention period without trial, which was extended to 90 days following the coup: less than a year later, largely due to European pressure, the detention period was reduced to 45 days. (162) While the military courts were incapable of coping with the overwhelming amount of cases and thousands were detained, this was also a legal gesture to Europe. Evren explains that "the detention period was too long and they wanted to reduce it even earlier, but in order not to be seen as submissive to European pressure, they postponed it. (163) However the question that needs to be answered is why they did not postpone it further when they needed to. A similar pattern of behaviour can be observed in another case. Under the military regime, the minimum conviction period to appeal in the high courts was increased to 36 months. The European institutions, particularly the EP and the Council of Europe, was pressing for its reduction. When Evren was asked to reduce it to 6 months by a representative of the Parliamentary Assembly he said " they would do so because the period was really too long but the Europeans must not think that it was because of European pressure." (164)

As the above examples show, the military regime and its head, Evren, were anxious not to be seen yielding to foreign pressure. Nonetheless, this over-sensitivity is also a sign that the European pressure was there and having an effect on the regime. It is very interesting to note Evren's reaction to European debates on the situation in Turkey. When the Parliamentary Assembly postponed the decision about the expulsion of Turkey from its October to its January session, Evren noted in his dairy "now we have gained three more months". On another occasion, when told by his advisers that the expulsion from the Council of Europe was unlikely, he wrote that, "the news relaxes me a bit". (165) This shows the generals' dilemma. On the one hand they wanted to restructure the whole political, legal and administrative system as they saw fit but, on the other hand, they could not practically do so independent of Europe. The European factor in this respect was always at least a reminder for the generals. This affected the whole procedure and timing of the return to civilian rule. In fact, Evren, in his memoirs noted that when they handed over power after the November general elections in 1983 " they thought the job was not finished yet". (166) The question emerges, then, as to why they handed power to a civilian government when there was no significant popular, more importantly open, internal opposition to the military regime. In fact, there was no external pressure on the regime other than from European. US was the only country that could influence the military rulers into a speedy return to civilian rule but due to security considerations US did not employ such policy on Turkey. On the contrary, it gave its full support and improved its relations with Ankara during the military regime. Therefore, the absence of such a demand for a return to democracy at home and abroad left European, particularly the EC and The Council of Europe, as the only sources of pressure.

It is unlikely that without such pressure the military would have handed over power to a civilian government in three years. In particular, the EC pressure and diplomacy played a crucial role in speeding up the transitional period and the transfer of power to a civilian government. However, the Community could not play the same role in shaping the democratisation process. Thus, after the civilian government came to power, the EC did not stop pressing for democratic reforms, but employed the same policy in a different form.

9) The European Influence on Turkish Politics and Democratisation, 1983 – 1990: Civilian Government and the EC

When a civilian government came to power following the November 1983 general elections, Turkey's relations with the EC were in deep crisis. This was mainly due to pre-election political developments. Since the EC could not impose its will in shaping pre-election democratic reforms, the EC as a whole, and particularly the EP, tended to continue its critical stance and press for further democratisation. Aware of the situation, the Ozal government declared its priorities to be the improvement of its relations with Europe and to join the EC. (167)

Despite this intention the government position was not seen as adequate for the improvement of relations with the EC. The opposition parties blamed the government for not being open enough and taking the necessary steps towards membership of the EC. The leader of the opposition party, the MDP, ex-general Turgut Suralp described the EC as the third most important economic, political and military pact adding that "Turkey cannot afford to leave Greece in this pack alone". (168) The leading member of the other opposition party, the HP, Erol Agagil, in a parliamentary speech urged the government to improve relations with Europe or face the consequences. In his emotional speech he noted that "the Ottoman Empire collapsed, the day it cut its ties with Europe", (169) The civilian government was, therefore, destined to be sensitive to European criticism, and this naturally led to European influence on progress towards democratisation.

Turkey's political presence in European quarters and its special relations with the EC were regarded as important element in reinforcing both Turkey's good image abroad and its fragile democracy at home. Therefore, the Ozal government was more than ready to co-operate and even compromise, to satisfy the European organisations in terms of political and legal reforms. To this effect the first Ozal government's foreign policy towards Europe was, in fact, an extension of that of the previous regime, with a more ambitious and co-operative manner, in terms of democratisation vis-à-vis European demands and influence.

However, contrary to Turkey's expectations, European criticism and demands moved from a broad reference to democracy and human rights to specific policies and legal reforms. As will shown, the civilian government had taken European criticism very seriously as it carried out further democratic reforms. Specific examples for the above approach can be found in both the government and opposition parties' statements and policy initiatives. For example, the deputy leader of the opposition party, Koksal Toptan, claimed in a parliamentary speech that "if his party was to govern, Turkey would join the EC because they would introduce democratic reforms immediately". (170) He also added that Turkey should immediately remove all those undemocratic political restrictions which Europeans have difficulties in understanding. This, he said " would accelerate our membership, otherwise we would fall apart from the EC". (171) Moreover, when Vahit Halefoglu, the Foreign Secretary, came to the chair to answer the opposition, he thanked it for its stance and expressed his government commitment to the cause.

This clearly reveals that the common view among Turkish politicians was that Turkey was lacking a true democracy and thus democratic reforms needed to be introduced and furthermore that without a full democracy Turkish membership of the EC was not imminent. Therefore, European concerns on the issues of democracy and human rights were regarded as genuine and legitimate, and it was accepted that Turkey needed to satisfy the Europeans in terms of democracy and human rights if it wished to join the EC. More importantly, these views were shared by all the mainstream parties and civil organisations such as trade unions, press, associations, human reights organisations and other NGOs. (172) On the other hand, Europeans were aware of the situation in Turkey, and they were convinced that their criticism was having a positive impact on the democratisation process and the improvement of the human rights situation in the country. It was, for example, argued by the European Parliamentarians that their appeal was effective in the provisional release of the detained president and six other members of the Turkish Peace Association, the trial of whom had caused strong reactions in Europe.

This point was to be proved correct by later developments. As the evidence shows, Ozal discussed such internal matters with the European delegations, which visited Turkey and gave information to officials as well as parliamentarians about Turkish human rights policy in his trips to the European capitals. (173) Ozal, as a pragmatic politician did not hesitate to discuss these matters openly with his European counterparts or other lower rank politicians. For example, he discussed the human rights situation and the issue of an amnesty with the delegations of PACE and promised to lift martial law further, reduce the detention period and reform the law of prosecution and execution. (174)

Despite the fact that, as his predecessors had done, Ozal sometimes publicly rejected European interference, behind closed doors he kept discussing matters in detail with the EC and other European officials and politicians. For example, when the EC criticised Turkey for new legislation, which increased the power of the police, Ozal publicly condemned the EC for interfering in Turkish internal affairs saying that "the EC had no right to comment on, or oppose a bill being debated by the Turkish Parliament". (175) However, despite his defiant stance, Ozal himself and government officials discussed the matter with EC officials and provided them with information about the proposed legislation. On the other hand, when the PACE initially declared that it would block the re-admission of the Turkish delegation, the Ozal government responded by threatening to leave the Assembly altogether. Accordingly, the Turkish Parliamentarians left the Assembly meeting in protest at the decision. (176) Both actions were severely criticised in the Turkish Parliament and the government was accused of being unrealistic in its reaction and was urged by deputies to compromise with the Council of Europe. (177) Ironically, both the government's defiant action against the Council of Europe and the Turkish Assembly's reaction to this indicate Turkish sensitivity to European criticism and the European impact on the Turkish policy-making bodies. Despite the fact that the Assembly was only pressing for further democratisation and the expulsion issue was not on the table, Ozal's statement was not more than a political manoeuvre and the opposition parties knew that. They took the opportunity to push the government into a corner and score points against it.

In this period, the government's main strategy was to gain European support and gradually normalise its relations with EC. Accordingly, when the government controlled Parliamentary Committee for Interior Affairs prepared a limited amnesty proposal which both the EC and the Council of Europe had been pushing for, it was widely publicised in European Capitals by Turkish Parliamentarians and diplomats. The aim of this campaign was particularly to impress the members of the PACE before its May session, at which Turkey hoped to re-establish the representation of its parliamentary group. (178) Due to European pressure and Ozal's willingness to establish his government's legitimacy abroad, Ozal decided to bring the local election date forward. He also abolished the law enacted by the previous military regime to prevent former politicians from taking part in the elections, which was another controversial issue between Turkey and the European quarters. The Europeans interpreted this as a move to establish his government's legitimacy in Turkey as much as an attempt to promote Turkey's image in the eyes of the Europeans. (179)

The allegations of torture and deteriorating prison conditions in the country were major issues between Turkey and Europe. The Turkish government was continuously asked to bring an end to these abuses. As part of its new strategy the Ozal government took the issue seriously and, in response to these allegations, a parliamentary committee was established in 1985 to investigate them. It is worth noting that the Chair of the committee, his deputy and some other members of the committee were also in the Turkish delegation to the PACE. It is not a coincidence that the committee was set up by the MPs who had contacts with the European Parliamentarians and had been officially representing Turkey in European platforms. Therefore, one can argue that the committee was more a response to the European critics of human rights, an information gathering centre to defend the human rights record of Turkey against outside critics, rather than a purely internal reformist move. With these positive steps taking place, the government was doing whatever it could to improve Turkey's image in Europe. For the European pressure, the blame was again publicly put on the Turkish Marxists and other leftist groups who were thought to be affecting the European politicians as well as public opinion of Europe.

However, in general terms, the Turkish government acknowledged the European influence. Therefore responding to European pressure it promised to improve prison conditions and to reform the administration of prisons. The Ozal government also started to introduce a new democratisation programme, which included the improvement of human rights and prison conditions. (180) The main characteristic of this period was that European criticism focused on specific allegations on human rights abuses and undemocratic practices particularly in the Eastern and South East part of the country. The allegations were that, despite the formal return to civilian rule, human rights violations continued to be systematic throughout the country. (181). Some argued that the allegations of torture and cruel treatment in police stations, prisons and military barracks even increased after the civilian government took office. Although this argument reflected the harsh reality, it did not necessarily mean that there was an increase in torture cases. On the contrary, the continuation of the democratisation programme and gradual lifting of martial law enabled the press and the people who were subject to torture or cruel treatment to raise their voice more freely and openly. This situation also encouraged human rights activists and the press to investigate and publish information about human rights abuses in the country. Under the previous military period it was only possible to do this from abroad in a limited capacity. In this period, the prosecution of some individual torturers was intentionally made public by the government, which also highlighted the human rights situation in the country. (182)

All the indications show that the Ozal government understood that the improvement of Turkey's relations with Europe was dependent on developments in the fields of democratisation and human rights. Furthermore, the Ozal government received full support from the main opposition parties in regard to improving relations with Europe. (183). The press, trade unions, large bussiness corporations and other civil organisations also supported the government in this policy. Enjoying unprecedented support, it took two significant steps in order to improve Turkey's image in Europe before its application for full membership of the EC. Preparing for an application the Turkish government felt obliged to make a gesture before it entered the discussions. The EC had been pressing for a general amnesty for a long time along with further democratisation. However, it was almost impossible for the Ozal government to introduce a general amnesty while Evren was President and maintaining his adamant stance against the general amnesty. In Evren's view such an action would have undermined the whole process of re-organisation which had started under the military regime and more importantly would have undermined the credibility of the military. Aware of the situation, Ozal cleverly introduced a limited amnesty for prisoners covering ordinary and political prisoners alike through an amendment of the execution law, which did not require presidential approval. As was expected, with the amendment almost all of the controversial prisoners of the Peace Association, DISK and some other journalists and writers who were in the centre of the dispute between Turkey and the EC were released. (184) The second step was to lift the ban on former politicians, which had also been a central focus of EC pressure on Turkey. These steps were particularly taken to please the EP and the Commission before Turkey's application for the EC membership was submitted. In line with the government, even Evren admitted that the Europeans were giving Ankara a hard time because of these trials and the political ban on the former politicians. (185)

The vital point in these developments, however, was Turkey's expectation of resuming the presidency of the Council of Europe and the normalisation of the relations with EC by re-activating the EC- Turkey Association Agreement. It is also important to note that the concessions were also in compliance with Turkey's recent promise to some member states particularly after the friendly settlement in ECHR. They were also response to the internal demand for democratisation. Since the military's harsh policies had been gradually relaxed the people, mainly human rights activities and leftist groups, had started to campaign for an improvement in the human rights situation and further democratisation. This was quite obvious when Evren angrily admitted that the last changes, particularly the partial amnesty, were carried out " under the influence of leftist campaigns in Turkey and in the West, which led to the release of many prisoners". (186) Evren admitted this to the Secretary General of the Council of Europe, Mr. M. Oreja, when he visited Turkey and urged the Secretary General not to believe the campaign against Turkey but to look at the facts. (187)

European pressure and influence increased after Turkey applied for accession into the EC. The Turkish government and Premier Ozal himself acknowledged this. (188) All the evidence shows that after Turkey's application in April 1987, criticism about Turkey's political fitness to join the EC increased. The application made Turkey more vulnerable than ever and its democratisation process and human rights situation come under the spotlight and under the scrutiny of the European public. This enabled the Europeans to base their judgements on a European standard and justify their claims on the basis that a candidate must comply with the basic European rules and uphold continental values.

The most important aspect of this process, however, was not European criticism but Turkey's defensive position. In practice by making the application, Turkey was submitting itself to the European scrutiny. While the application enabled the EC to impose its rule on Turkish domestic politics and scrutinise and monitor the legal and political developments, Turkey became more submissive, trying to prove its good intentions by taking more steps towards democratisation. Turkey's aim was to convince the EC that it was trying to establish a European political system in the country. This was also made public by the Secretary of State in charge of the EC Affairs when he stated that Turkey's decision to apply for accession was based on Turkey's desire "to live in a world of peace and security respectful of democracy and fundamental rights and freedoms like member states". (189)

As is indicated in the above statement and in many similar remarks, the membership of the EC, at least in theory, meant democratisation and respect of human rights in the country. If this was the case, and the application was based on enduring democracy and human rights, then Turkey had to conform to those principles in practice as a pre-condition set by the EC. This was clearly understood and accepted by the Turkish government as well as by the state elite including the military. This point was obvious in Ozal's 14 April 1987 press conference on the application. Ozal's prior concern was to prove that Turkey was politically fit to join the EC as a full member. Therefore, most of his speech explained the democratisation process, which was implemented following the military regime under his leadership. He went into details explaining the steps that Turkey had taken in the fields of democratisation and human rights. To prove Turkey's political fitness and its determination to be a modern democratic country he referred to the confirmation of Turkey's Europeanness at the European organisations and internal positive political developments regarding human rights and democracy. Premier Ozal proudly pointed to Turkey's readmittance to the Parliamentary Assembly and the Turkish Presidency of the Council of Europe. He also talked about the friendly settlement in ECHR as confirmation of Turkey's improving human rights record. According to him the five European states had dropped their charges against Turkey as a result of the successful democratisation programme and the improving human rights situation in the country. Alongside the above positive points, Ozal added his government's courage in accepting the right of individual petition to the ECHR. All these examples were given as evidence of Turkey's determination to catch up with European standards. He concluded that Turkey was politically and economically fit and ready for full membership of the EC. (190)

The above argument, which was officially presented by Premier Ozal on behalf of Turkey, clearly indicates Turkey's defensive position in its relations with the EC. This was of course due to the EC's pre-condition of democratisation and respect for human rights and Turkey's political fitness for its membership of the EC. Since this was understood clearly by the Turkish politicians in almost all attempts Turkish politicians anxiously referred to Turkey's several political, economic and military ties with Europe and tried to legitimise their argument by giving reference to other European organisations. Ozal, for example, in September 1987 claimed that the acceptance of the ruling Motherland Party as a member of the International Democratic Union showed that there was no human rights problem in Turkey. (191). In this respect, Turkey used its presidency of the Council of Europe to its advantage when it submitted its application for accession. Furthermore, following the application, the Turkish government openly indicated that it would collaborate with European institutions on the issues of democracy and human rights. To show its good will, it gave permission to an Amnesty International Team on the same day of the application to study prison conditions in Turkey. (192) With the application the Turkish elite became aware of the restraint put on Turkish domestic politics, which led to two dimensions in the policy-making and implementation process.

First, the Turkish government willingly accepted the new European dimension in Turkey's internal policies, which obliged the government to commit itself to be more transparent in furthering the democratisation programme and improving the human rights situation in the country. (193) Secondly, the Turkish government had to accept the increased interest of European public opinion in Turkish domestic politics and the legitimacy of European interference in its domestic affairs. While the application enabled each member country to interfere in Turkey's domestic affairs alongside the international European organisations, the Turkish government, and to a large extent, the Turkish elite, including the military, started to embrace the reality that Turkey required the condition of a country seeking to join a club to be checked before admittance. This was clearly observed even in military circles. Evren, as Head of State and a symbol of the military influence in Turkish politics acknowledged the fact that Turkey's bid for membership of the EC increased European pressure on Turkey. Even when he criticised the human rights activists he indicated his acceptance of the pressure on Turkey by stating that "if we want to join the EC what can we do but put up with them {Europeans}". (194)

Political developments clearly proved that the Turkish government became concerned about the standard of human rights and democracy in the country and the fact that these did not meet European standards. This suggested that the Turkish government had to take decisive steps in the direction of closing the gap. An important example of such a policy was the Ozal government's acceptance of individual petition to the ECHR in January 1987. This was in fact a political gesture by Ankara to show that it was totally committed to improving the human rights situation in the country and trying to catch up with European standards in this area. However, the official government announcement on the issue suggested that it was a move by the government to improve image of the country in Europe rather than a commitment to improve the human rights situation in the country. After the decision the government issued a statement through its spokesman Secretary of State H. Gelal Guzel which clearly stated the above concern. In the statement Mr. Guzel stated that, after the government's acceptance of the right of individuals to apply to ECHR, that this decision would contribute to Turkey's relations with Europe. (195)

Despite the above statement, which clearly indicates the European dimension and the hope that the decision would have a positive effect on the EC-Turkey relations, Ozal denied any suggestion that the government took the decision under any domestic or external pressure. However, the evidence proved the opposite. There was, in fact, a European Parliament resolution calling on the Turkish government to accept the right of individual appeal to the ECHR. Furthermore, the timing of the decision, which was two months before the membership application was submitted, and the official statements following its ratification suggested that the decision was not a separate individual case but it was a part of an ongoing democratisation and image-making process that was embarked on by the Turkish government on the eve of its application for full membership. Turkey's effort to repair its damaged prestige and show the EC that Turkey was politically fit to join the club continued after the application.

In this respect, following the application for accession, the Turkish government took two further steps in order to show its commitment to the democratisation process. First, the long-criticised internal exile law was abolished one day after the application was made on 15 April 1987. Second, Ozal announced on April 28 1987, that a draft constitutional amendment to lift the constitutional ban on former political leaders was to be submitted by his party. (196). This announcement ironically showed the change of attitude on the side of the military establishment, and President Evren. The lifting of the constitutional ban on former politicians by abolishing, Article 4, which required Presidential approval, had long been opposed by the military and President Evren despite the internal and European pressure. Evren explained that he was considering lifting the ban in mid 1986 but after consultation with his military colleges, he decided to abandon the idea. (197) This highlights the military involvement in Turkish politics as well as Evren's collaboration with the military despite his presidential post.

As explained above throughout the referendum on Article 4 Ozal and his party campaigned for a no vote despite their initial call for liberalisation of the Turkish political system. However, after the referendum, Ozal tried to capitalise on the result as a significant step towards the democratisation and liberalisation of the country. The Turkish government expected the Europeans to ease their criticism of Turkey after the referendum. In this respect, when the Turkish Minister for the EC Affairs met with the President of the Council of Foreign Ministers of the EC, he stated that the EC should no longer criticise the Turkish regime for being undemocratic and relations between the two parties should be totally normalised. Ozal's aim to capitalise on the result of the referendum was also shared by some Europeans. For example, William Hale argued that the result of the referendum would improve "the modest chance of success of Turkey's recent application for membership of the EC". (198)

Another striking example of the impact of the EC on Turkish internal politics was illustrated when Evren warned the government and the state elites against the growing "reactionary forces" in the country. After Evren's warning, Universities, under the direction of the Higher Education Authority (*Yuksek Ogretim Kurumu-YOK*) introduced a ban on the use of headscarf within university campuses in May 1987. While Evren became champion of the ban, Ozal took a different stand and openly linked the ban to Turkey's application for membership of the EC. In contrast to Evren's stand and the universities' practice Premier Ozal said " at a time when Turkey as a democratic country, has applied for full membership in the EC, blowing the issue of what people should wear out of all proportion disturbs me very much". (199) Two different factors can easily be read in these statements. First, the importance of the EC factor in Turkish domestic politics. Secondly, the state elite's concerns about EC membership and the impact of the application on Turkish domestic politics. However, Ozal was not successful in this matter. The headscarf ban was imposed -and is still in force- by the state's elite who were openly backed up by the military establishment despite government disapproval.

Somehow, unlike other undemocratic practices, this particular policy was not criticized by the EC. As the EC had been putting pressure on the government in relation to the lack of democracy and the human rights situation in the country, and raising specific issues such as trials of the members of Peace Association and DISK as well as the ban on Communist Party the silence of Europe on the issue of the headscarf can be interpreted as double standards by the Europeans. It can be argued that in this particular issue France may have influenced the EC, because of the attitude taken by the French authorities to Islamic identity by French school children. However, while the EC kept its silence on the issue of the headscarf, at the same time it showed a totally different attitude towards the ban on the communist party.

Due to European pressure the Turkish government showed same relaxation with regard to lifting the ban on the formation of a communist party. This was because the Turkish government recognised its difficulties in improving the relations with Europe while keeping the ban. Ozal pointed this out in March 1987 just one month before the application was lodged. When he argued that in the process of the integration into Europe through the EC, Turkey should and would adopt a more liberal political system which required dropping the ban on the formation of a Communist Party. In his televised speech Ozal also pointed out that even if the ban were lifted with immediate effect, the people of Turkey would favour neither the Islamic nor the communist parties. Therefore, according to him, lifting the ban would not pose any danger to the state.

However, if there was no demand for an Islamist or a Communist Party at home, why should the government rush to lift the ban? As later came to light, Ozal was aware of the EC stand on the issue and was concerned about the possible harm that might be inflicted on Turkey's relations with the EC by the ban.

For the same reasons, Ozal government gradually initiated a softer approach to the Kurdish issue which had been a source of irritation in the relations between Turkey and the EC for a long time, particularly after 1985. The government in its new approach indicated that Kurdish ethnicity might be recognised only on cultural matters. Nevertheless, the government did not intend to recognise -and still does not recognise- the Kurdish people as a minority. Even this modest approach, however, created a hostile debate in the country. While Ozal and his government were accused of being separatist (at least inflicting a separatist idea among the public) by the opposition forces, who were mainly nationalists and Kemalists, the issue was again clearly linked to the Turkish application for the full membership of the EC. This became apparent when Evren condemned the Europeans for their critical stance. In his words the Europeans were " using the Armenian and Kurdish issue like the sword of Damocles over our heads". (200)

On the other hand, the Turkish government conducted a concentrated campaign to show its determination in changing the perceived European attitude towards Turkey, using diplomatic and even commercial means. To this end the government employed some prominent advertising companies for a campaign to change the image of Turkey in the eyes of the European public. The new strategy had two aspects. One was to organise meetings and conferences for the western envoys in Ankara and in the western capitals for the European politicians in order to explain the Turkish government's determination to fight against human rights abuse and implement the necessary legal and political reforms to further the democratisation. Secondly, these meetings and conferences were used to answer the claims of the international human rights organisations notably Amnesty International.

Under this new strategy, the Turkish government abandoned its original defiant stance and committed itself to explaining the improvements, which had been made since the civil government came to power. Contrary to its initial stance, the Turkish government began to realise the effect of the non-governmental human rights organisations on Western public opinion and governments. It therefore, initiated a strategy to counter-attack the claims of these circles rather than to ignore them, as was the case during the military regime and in the early years of the civilian government. For example, expressing his concerns over the reports of Amnesty International on Turkey, Ozal stated that "they may have a negative effect on our foreign affairs whether they reflect the reality or not". (201) A spokesman for the Turkish Foreign Ministry voiced similar opinions when he responded to a specific report of the Amnesty International, stating: " I hope the report will not effect the relations between the EC and Turkey". (202) The main reason for Turkey in taking AI reports seriously and counter-attacking their claims was the belief that the reports were not only harming Turkey's image in Europe, but also affecting the European governments approaches towards Turkey.

Thus, it was believed that the AI's reports on Turkey might reduce Turkey's chance for accession to the EC. The Turkish government also believed that AI was trying to influence the European governments and the Commission of the EC by publishing its reports on human rights violations in Turkey on the eve of the Commission's decision on Turkey's application. This was clearly indicated in Evren's announcement that " the allegations of torture were aimed to prevent the Turkish membership of the EC". (203) However, as a counter-attack, the Turkish government had always claimed that torturers were being tried and strongly denied any systematic torture allegations. (204) It is worth mentioning that the direct response of the Turkish government to the reports of AI increased after the Turkish application for full membership. For instance, for the first time the Turkish government fully investigated the 229 death cases, which were mentioned in the AI briefing in November 1988. Furthermore, Ankara reported back to AI on 174 cases admitting ill treatment in 41 cases. (205) The Ozal government also responded to other specific torture and ill-treatment allegations raised by AI and other bodies. Ankara's direct response to AI and other European based human rights organisations clearly indicated that the Turkish government was not only counter-attacking the allegations of torture and other human rights abuses but also becoming more open to listen to any criticism and more willing to investigate the claims. Because Ankara was concern about the possible negative effect of the AI reports on Turkey's application for full membership of the EC the government chose to listen to the critics and tried to persuade them to change their views rather than ignoring them.

With this aim, the Ozal government decided to undertake international legal commitments such as the European and UN conventions against torture which were both signed in January 1988 and respectively ratified in February and August of the same year. This meant that Turkey accepted the authority of independent teams to investigate torture complaints and prison conditions in the country without the permission of the Turkish authorities. Indeed, Turkey was the first country to ratify the European anti-torture Convention despite the fact that it was the last to sign it. However, Premier Ozal used the occasion to express his government's determination to promote and protect human rights in the country. The ratification of the conventions was praised both by politicians and the Turkish media. The Foreign Minister specifically praised the ratification of the conventions and commented on their important place in Turkey's foreign affairs.

In a wider analysis, however, one can easily claim that Turkey was using the ratification of the conventions to promote its image in Europe as well as using them as a sweetener for European concerns with regard to the current and future appraisal of the human rights situation. As Dagi argued " the move targeted the outside audience not the domestic concern" (206). In fact at the time of allegations of torture, the government wanted to pre-empt the criticisms and persuade the Europeans about Turkey's commitment to improve the human rights conditions in the country. (207) Indeed the motive behind the sudden change of behaviour by the Turkish government and the sudden ratification of the conventions was no more than an attempt to enhance Turkey's position in its bid for accession to the EC. Ankara's aim was to give a clear indication to the Commission before its decision on Turkey's application. Ozal's New Year Message of 1989 claimed that the previous twelve months had been a "landmark" against torture by which " the western standards of human rights had begun to be applied". However, the question of how and to what extent to allow the independent teams from Europe to inspect the Turkish prisons and police stations, which would be a "landmark" event, was not answered in the statement. In fact, to declare these ratifications as a "landmark" for Turkish democracy can only tell us that the Turkish government was too anxious to prove its democratic credentials to the Europeans. Thus, the whole scenario of the diplomacy and media statements by Premier Ozal and other government officials suggested a determined decision by the government to highlight the ratification of the conventions as a public relations exercise to allow any concerns the EC may have concerning Turkish admission to the EC. In fact the whole scenario and the importance the government attached to the ratification and the government's intensive diplomacy and high profile policy to publicise the move abroad can only suggest that the move was neither a natural commitment following democratic principles nor addressed to domestic problems. Instead it can be suggested that the move aimed to improve Turkey's image in Europe by pre-empting possible accusations.

In line with the above approach the government decided to introduce a legal reform package which reduced the death penalty offences from 29 to 13. Other notable changes were to reduce the period of detention without charge from 15 days to 24 hours and to increase the access of lawyers to detainees. (208) The timing of the move and the announcement was aimed to please the Europeans rather than to meet Turkey's internal requirements. Ozal announced the government's decision in September 1989 before he declared Turkey's acceptance of the compulsory jurisdiction of the Council of Europe. (209) The Ankara's crusade against the so-called propaganda on Turkey's human rights record was backed up by the legal and administrative reforms which was designed to strengthen the government position in Europe. It is worth noting that the legal reforms and changes were mostly in areas on which European critics concentrated and were a response to European demands.

In the last attempt to convince the Europeans about the internal improvements and the Government's determination to improve human rights practices to European standards, Ozal himself took the case to Europe in September, just two months before the Commission submitted its opinion to the Council of Ministers of the EC. In his speech, Ozal specifically highlighted Turkey's acceptance of the Compulsory Jurisdiction of the European Court of Human Rights and other reforms that had been carried out by his government. In his view Turkey had done its job and prepared for the membership of the EC. At the end of his speech Ozal asked for full support from the members of the Parliamentary Assembly. (210)

As has been shown, in this period Ankara tended to be more receptive to European criticism than ever before. Ozal, in defending Ankara's receptiveness, claimed that his government took all logical and acceptable criticism seriously. For this reason Ozal promised to establish a human rights section in the Prime Minister's office and a similar committee in Parliament. (211) According to Dagi, for this particular project the impetus came from Eyyup Asik and Bulent Akarcali. Both MPs were members of the Turkish delegations in the Parliamentary Assembly of the Council of Europe and Turkey-EC Joint Parliamentary Committee. The Human Rights Committee came into existence in December 1990. The president of the Committee Eyyup Asik in an interview admitted that Foreign Ministry bureaucrats and the Turkish parliamentarians who were in contact with the Europeans were influenced by the European human rights activists, and they passed these views on to the Turkish government and Turkish politicians. (212) As he put it "once a deputy returns home from a trip to Europe, he becomes a staunch defender of human rights. This is the issue they talked about everywhere. Although we get angry with them, we are glad too, because they make us do good things."(213)

This might be an extraordinary admission but it reflects reality: the degree of European influence and Turkish receptiveness. Another important factor in the establishment of the committee, which was meant to investigate alleged human rights abuses in the country, was the full support of the Turkish Ministry of Foreign Affairs. The Turkish foreign ministry's interest and direct involvement and full support reveals that human rights issues were considered a foreign policy problem rather than a matter for internal reform. The above developments leave no doubt about European influence on the Turkish politicians and bureaucrats alike. In contrast to this, Ozal maintained that the Turkish people wished for progress in political liberalisation and stability in the country and that the reforms and the democratisation process were the result of this popular wish. However, he proudly expressed his view that the European Parliament and other European organisations acknowledged the democratic credentials of the regime in the country and added "they have improved Turkey's democratic image abroad."(214)

10) Conclusion

This study has shown that Turkey's place in Europe and its human rights record had not been questioned during the Cold War period. Turkey's indispensable strategic value for the West prevented the Europeans from questioning Turkey's European credentials until the late 1980s. The issue was not significantly raised even when Turkey signed the Ankara Agreement with the EEC in 1963, which envisaged a possible full membership. Even the emergence of human rights issues in world politics in the late 1970s did not significantly change the European stance against Turkey. Instead, in line with the US permissive policy towards friendly states, Turkey was not confronted by the EC or by the member-states. Only after the 1980 military coup in Turkey, Europeans and particularly the EC, started to question Turkey's democratic credentials and demand the immediate return to civilian rule and the upholding of European political principles and values. This in itself implies that Turkey was regarded as being on the periphery of Europe. However, despite the presence of a civilian government and considerable democratic reforms in the late 1980s and 1990s, Europe still questioned Turkey's 'Europeanness'. This can be explained largely by the lessening tension in East-West relations. However, this approach did not lead to a total breakdown in the relations between Turkey and the EC. On the contrary it gave an impulse to Turkey to explain itself to the EC, which at the same time increased European influence on Turkey. This is directly related to Turkey's ideological, cultural, economic and political linkages to Europe.

In line with the above trend, the EC started to impose pressure on Turkey regarding its human rights record and lack of democracy. Between 1980 and 1983 the EC pressure mainly aimed to accelerate the return to civil rule and the return to civilian rule was influenced by EC. The EC played an important positive role in the process by employing diplomatic, political and economic means. In the second phase, between 1983 and 1990, the same policy intensified in order to accelerate the general democratisation process in the country and bring an end to alleged human rights abuses. In this period the EC highlighted particular issues and pressurised the Turkish government for solutions.

Although, the level and kind of EC pressure in forms of economic and political means was an important factor in returning to civil rule and in the later democratisation process, the vital factor was, in fact, Turkey's co-operative and receptive policy, which was a result of Turkey's strong linkages with the EC. This was, to large extent, the motivating reason for the internal demand for democratisation. In fact, the success of a policy of pressure is dependent on the degree of the linkages that the subject state has with the centres of pressure and to the importance attached to them. As has been argued, Turkey has ideologically identified itself with Europe and found indispensable military, economic and political benefits in the continuation of its relations with the EC. Furthermore, Turkey's strong aspiration to become part of the EC inevitably created the possibility for the Community to influence a policy change regarding democracy and human rights in Turkey between 1980 and 1990. Turkey's aspiration to become a full member of the EC is now perceived by the ruling elite, civil and military alike, and largely by the intelligentsia as achievable only through further democratisation and the improvement of the human rights situation in the country.

It has also been shown that the European factor was the most important driving force in the whole democratisation programme and in the implementation of the legal and administrative reforms in both phases: 1980-1983 and 1983-1990. During the military period the European constraints and influence on the military rulers effected the return to civilian rule. Similarly, European pressure on the civilian government between 1983 and 1990 played a constructive role in the process of liberalisation of the political system and in the improving of the human rights situation in the country. This was particularly the case after the membership application. The government, in fact the whole military and civil elite, became aware that Turkey needed to liberalise its political system and improve the human rights situation if it wanted to join the EC. Furthermore, it was clearly understood that Turkey's application was dependent on its success in the fields of democratisation and human rights. With this is in mind, the Ozal government speeded up the process of democratisation and introduced a set of economic, legal, political and social reforms which all aimed to improve Turkey's image in Europe and boost its bid for full membership.

On the other hand, Turkey's application for full membership started a new process which gave the EC a chance to set its rules for accession and gave Turkey time and space to comply with these rules. This not only enabled the EC to interfere in Turkish domestic affairs but also made Turkish domestic policy dependent on Turkey's relations with the EC. As the government declared membership of the EC as its foreign policy priority, the political reforms particularly in the fields of human rights and the liberalisation of the Turkish political and justice system should be considered in the context of the European dimension in Turkish politics. This priority goal, which was also upheld by the main opposition parties, naturally had direct implications on Turkish domestic and foreign policies.

The administration was aware that the current parliamentary democracy was insufficient and that a more liberal, more democratic regime based on respect for human rights was the precondition for Turkey's acceptance into the EC. This was, in fact, a source of encouragement and at the same time constraint for the Turkish government with regard to democratisation reforms and human rights policies. For the civilian government it was a source of strength to explain itself and its policies to the military and the statist establishments. This was, indeed, adopted as a common strategy by almost all the politicians in the country. For example, the main opposition party leader claimed that if they won the forthcoming election and became a government, they would succeed in winning EC full membership for Turkey as they would improve the human rights situation in the country. (215) As is obvious from the above statement, even the Turkish politicians' own assessment the chance for admission to the EC was simply based on the degree of Turkey's success in implementing democratic reforms and improving the human rights situation in the country. This factor was highlighted by the meeting of the Turkish Foreign Minister and the European Affairs Minister with the Turkish Ambassadors in the 12 EC countries. (216)

However, the more important point was the Turkish government's stance. The Turkish government also continuously informed the Europeans about the internal developments and urged them to take into consideration the political liberalisation and improvements in the fields of human rights that were achieved by Turkey. As Turkey asked the Europeans to "rate" its domestic developments, this naturally gave considerable leverage to Europeans to influence the whole process. This is acknowledged in a European Parliament resolution, which emphasised that "under the influence of Europe, present-day of Turkey has established a constitution and legal system on the model of the Western European nations". (217)

Turkish governments in general have been happy to be "rated" in order to secure accession to the EC and have shown readiness to do more to achieve this goal.

This reasoning can also be seen in other policies proposed or implemented by the Turkish government. The framework of the EU - Turkish relationship established between 1980 and 1990 remains in tact and as long as Turkey's full membership is on the table, thus the issues of human rights and democracy will continue to be at the core of the relations between Turkey and the EU for the foreseeable future.

UNIVERSAL DECLARATION OF HUMAN RIGHTS

The Universal Declaration of Human Rights (UDHR) is a milestone document in the history of human rights. Drafted by representatives with different legal and cultural backgrounds from all regions of the world, the Declaration was proclaimed by the United Nations General Assembly in Paris on 10 December 1948 as a common standard of achievements for all peoples and all nations. It sets out, for the first time, fundamental human rights to be universally protected.

Article 1.

- All human beings are born free and equal in dignity and rights. They are endowed with reason and conscience and should act towards one another in a spirit of brotherhood.

Article 2.

- Everyone is entitled to all the rights and freedoms set forth in this Declaration, without distinction of any kind, such as race, colour, sex, language, religion, political or other opinion, national or social origin, property, birth or other status. Furthermore, no distinction shall be made on the basis of the political, jurisdictional or international status of the country or territory to which a person belongs, whether it be independent, trust, non-self-governing or under any other limitation of sovereignty.

Article 3.

- Everyone has the right to life, liberty and security of person.

Article 4.

- No one shall be held in slavery or servitude; slavery and the slave trade shall be prohibited in all their forms.

Article 5.

- No one shall be subjected to torture or to cruel, inhuman or degrading treatment or punishment.

Article 6.

- Everyone has the right to recognition everywhere as a person before the law.

Article 7.

- All are equal before the law and are entitled without any discrimination to equal protection of the law. All are entitled to equal protection against any discrimination in violation of this Declaration and against any incitement to such discrimination.

Article 8.

- Everyone has the right to an effective remedy by the competent national tribunals for acts violating the fundamental rights granted him by the constitution or by law.

Article 9.

- No one shall be subjected to arbitrary arrest, detention or exile.

Article 10.

- Everyone is entitled in full equality to a fair and public hearing by an independent and impartial tribunal, in the determination of his rights and obligations and of any criminal charge against him.

Article 11.

- (1) Everyone charged with a penal offence has the right to be presumed innocent until proved guilty according to law in a public trial at which he has had all the guarantees necessary for his defence.
- (2) No one shall be held guilty of any penal offence on account of any act or omission which did not constitute a penal offence, under national or international law, at the time when it was committed. Nor shall a heavier penalty be imposed than the one that was applicable at the time the penal offence was committed.

Article 12.

- No one shall be subjected to arbitrary interference with his privacy, family, home or correspondence, nor to attacks upon his honour and reputation. Everyone has the right to the protection of the law against such interference or attacks.

Article 13.

- (1) Everyone has the right to freedom of movement and residence within the borders of each state.
- (2) Everyone has the right to leave any country, including his own, and to return to his country.

Article 14.

- (1) Everyone has the right to seek and to enjoy in other countries asylum from persecution.
- (2) This right may not be invoked in the case of prosecutions genuinely arising from non-political crimes or from acts contrary to the purposes and principles of the United Nations.

Article 15.

- (1) Everyone has the right to a nationality.
- (2) No one shall be arbitrarily deprived of his nationality nor denied the right to change his nationality.

Article 16.

- (1) Men and women of full age, without any limitation due to race, nationality or religion, have the right to marry and to found a family. They are entitled to equal rights as to marriage, during marriage and at its dissolution.
- (2) Marriage shall be entered into only with the free and full consent of the intending spouses.
- (3) The family is the natural and fundamental group unit of society and is entitled to protection by society and the State.

Article 17.

- (1) Everyone has the right to own property alone as well as in association with others.
- (2) No one shall be arbitrarily deprived of his property.

Article 18.

- Everyone has the right to freedom of thought, conscience and religion; this right includes freedom to change his religion or belief, and freedom, either alone or in community with others and in public or private, to manifest his religion or belief in teaching, practice, worship and observance.

Article 19.

- Everyone has the right to freedom of opinion and expression; this right includes freedom to hold opinions without interference and to seek, receive and impart information and ideas through any media and regardless of frontiers.

Article 20.

- (1) Everyone has the right to freedom of peaceful assembly and association.
- (2) No one may be compelled to belong to an association.

Article 21.

- (1) Everyone has the right to take part in the government of his country, directly or through freely chosen representatives.
- (2) Everyone has the right of equal access to public service in his country.
- (3) The will of the people shall be the basis of the authority of government; this will shall be expressed in periodic and genuine elections which shall be by universal and equal suffrage and shall be held by secret vote or by equivalent free voting procedures.

Article 22.

- Everyone, as a member of society, has the right to social security and is entitled to realization, through national effort and international co-operation and in accordance with the organization and resources of each State, of the economic, social and cultural rights indispensable for his dignity and the free development of his personality.

Article 23.

- (1) Everyone has the right to work, to free choice of employment, to just and favourable conditions of work and to protection against unemployment.
- (2) Everyone, without any discrimination, has the right to equal pay for equal work.
- (3) Everyone who works has the right to just and favourable remuneration ensuring for himself and his family an existence worthy of human dignity, and supplemented, if necessary, by other means of social protection.

- (4) Everyone has the right to form and to join trade unions for the protection of his interests.

Article 24.

- Everyone has the right to rest and leisure, including reasonable limitation of working hours and periodic holidays with pay.

Article 25.

- (1) Everyone has the right to a standard of living adequate for the health and well-being of himself and of his family, including food, clothing, housing and medical care and necessary social services, and the right to security in the event of unemployment, sickness, disability, widowhood, old age or other lack of livelihood in circumstances beyond his control.
- (2) Motherhood and childhood are entitled to special care and assistance. All children, whether born in or out of wedlock, shall enjoy the same social protection.

Article 26.

- (1) Everyone has the right to education. Education shall be free, at least in the elementary and fundamental stages. Elementary education shall be compulsory. Technical and professional education shall be made generally available and higher education shall be equally accessible to all on the basis of merit.
- (2) Education shall be directed to the full development of the human personality and to the strengthening of respect for human rights and fundamental freedoms. It shall promote understanding, tolerance and friendship among all nations, racial or religious groups, and shall further the activities of the United Nations for the maintenance of peace.
- (3) Parents have a prior right to choose the kind of education that shall be given to their children.

Article 27.

- (1) Everyone has the right freely to participate in the cultural life of the community, to enjoy the arts and to share in scientific advancement and its benefits.
- (2) Everyone has the right to the protection of the moral and material interests resulting from any scientific, literary or artistic production of which he is the author.

Article 28.

- Everyone is entitled to a social and international order in which the rights and freedoms set forth in this Declaration can be fully realized.

Article 29.

- (1) Everyone has duties to the community in which alone the free and full development of his personality is possible.
- (2) In the exercise of his rights and freedoms, everyone shall be subject only to such limitations as are determined by law solely for the purpose of securing due recognition and respect for the rights and freedoms of others and of meeting the just requirements of morality, public order and the general welfare in a democratic society.
- (3) These rights and freedoms may in no case be exercised contrary to the purposes and principles of the United Nations.

Article 30.

- Nothing in this Declaration may be interpreted as implying for any State, group or person any right to engage in any activity or to perform any act aimed at the destruction of any of the rights and freedoms set forth herein.

THE CORE INTERNATIONAL HUMAN RIGHTS INSTRUMENTS

and their monitoring bodies

THE INTERNATIONAL BILL OF HUMAN RIGHTS

- Universal Declaration of Human Rights 1948
- International Covenant on Economic, Social and Cultural Rights 1966
- International Covenant on Civil and Political Rights 1966
- Optional Protocol to the International Covenant on Civil and Political Rights
- Second Optional Protocol to the International Covenant on Civil and Political Rights, aiming at the abolition of the death penalty

THE CORE INTERNATIONAL HUMAN RIGHTS INSTRUMENTS and their monitoring bodies

There are nine core international human rights treaties. Each of these treaties has established a committee of experts to monitor implementation of the treaty provisions by its States parties. Some of the treaties are supplemented by optional protocols dealing with specific concerns.

		Date	Monitoring Body
ICERD	International Convention on the Elimination of All Forms of Racial Discrimination	21 Dec 1965	CERD
ICCPR	International Covenant on Civil and Political Rights	16 Dec 1966	CCPR
ICESCR	International Covenant on Economic, Social and Cultural Rights	16 Dec 1966	CESCR
CEDAW	Convention on the Elimination of All Forms	18	CEDAW

	of Discrimination against Women	Dec 1979	
CAT	Convention against Torture and Other Cruel, Inhuman or Degrading Treatment or Punishment	10 Dec 1984	CAT
CRC	Convention on the Rights of the Child	20 Nov 1989	CRC
ICRMW	International Convention on the Protection of the Rights of All Migrant Workers and Members of Their Families	18 Dec 1990	CMW
	International Convention for the Protection of All Persons from Enforced Disappearance	20 Dec 2006	
CRPD	Convention on the Rights of Persons with Disabilities	13 Dec 2006	CRPD
ICESCR - OP	Optional Protocol of the Covenant on Economic, Social and Cultural Rights	10 Dec 2008	CESCR
ICCPR-OP1	Optional Protocol to the International Covenant on Civil and Political Rights	16 Dec 1966	HRC
ICCPR-OP2	Second Optional Protocol to the International Covenant on Civil and Political Rights, aiming at the abolition of the death penalty	15 Dec 1989	HRC
OP-CEDAW	Optional Protocol to the Convention on the Elimination of Discrimination against Women	10 Dec 1999	CEDAW
OP-CRC-AC	Optional protocol to the Convention on the Rights of the Child on the involvement of children in armed conflict	25 May 2000	CRC
OP-CRC-SC	Optional protocol to the Convention on the Rights of the Child on the sale of children, child prostitution and child pornography	25 May 2000	CRC
OP-CAT	Optional Protocol to the Convention against Torture and Other Cruel, Inhuman or Degrad-	18 Dec	CAT

	ing Treatment or Punishment	2002	
OP-CRPD	Optional Protocol to the Convention on the Rights of Persons with Disabilities	12 Dec 2006	CRPD

UNIVERSAL HUMAN RIGHTS INSTRUMENTS

In addition to the International Bill of Rights and the core human rights treaties, there are many other universal instruments relating to human rights. A non-exhaustive selection is listed below. The legal status of these instruments varies: declarations, principles, guidelines, standard rules and recommendations have no binding legal effect, but such instruments have an undeniable moral force and provide practical guidance to States in their conduct; covenants, statutes, protocols and conventions are legally-binding for those States that ratify or accede to them. Information on the status of ratification selected instruments is available here.

WORLD CONFERENCE ON HUMAN RIGHTS AND MILLENNIUM ASSEMBLY

- Vienna Declaration and Programme of Action
- United Nations Millennium Declaration

THE RIGHT OF SELF-DETERMINATION

- United Nations Declaration on the Granting of Independence to Colonial Countries and Peoples
- General Assembly resolution 1803 (XVII) of 14 December 1962, "Permanent sovereignty over natural resources"
- International Convention against the Recruitment, Use, Financing and Training of Mercenaries

RIGHTS OF INDIGENOUS PEOPLES AND MINORITIES

- Declaration on the Rights of Indigenous Peoples

- Indigenous and Tribal Peoples Convention, 1989 (No. 169)
- Declaration on the Rights of Persons Belonging to National or Ethnic, Religious and Linguistic Minorities

PREVENTION OF DISCRIMINATION

- Equal Remuneration Convention, 1951 (No. 100)
- Discrimination (Employment and Occupation) Convention, 1958 (No. 111)
- International Convention on the Elimination of all Forms of Racial Discrimination (ICERD)
- Declaration on Race and Racial Prejudice
- Convention against Discrimination in Education
- Protocol Instituting a Conciliation and Good Offices Commission to be responsible for seeking a settlement of any disputes which may arise between States Parties to the Convention against Discrimination in Education
- Declaration on the Elimination of All Forms of Intolerance and of Discrimination Based on Religion or Belief
- World Conference against Racism, 2001 (Durban Declaration and Programme of Action)

RIGHTS OF WOMEN

- Convention on the Elimination of All Forms of Discrimination against Women (CEDAW)
- Optional Protocol to the Convention on the Elimination of All Forms of Discrimination against Women (CEDAW-OP)
- Declaration on the Protection of Women and Children in Emergency and Armed Conflict
- Declaration on the Elimination of Violence against Women

RIGHTS OF THE CHILD

- Convention on the Rights of the Child (CRC)

- Optional Protocol to the Convention on the Rights of the Child on the sale of children, child prostitution and child pornography (CRC-OPSC)
- Optional Protocol to the Convention on the Rights of the Child on the involvement of children in armed conflict (CRC-OPAC)
- Minimum Age Convention, 1973 (No. 138)
- Worst Forms of Child Labour Convention, 1999 (No. 182)

RIGHTS OF OLDER PERSONS

- United Nations Principles for Older Persons

RIGHTS OF PERSONS WITH DISABILITIES

- Declaration on the Rights of Mentally Retarded Persons
- Declaration on the Rights of Disabled Persons
- Principles for the protection of persons with mental illness and the improvement of mental health care
- Standard Rules on the Equalization of Opportunities for Persons with Disabilities

HUMAN RIGHTS IN THE ADMINISTRATION OF JUSTICE: PROTECTION OF PERSONS SUBJECTED TO DETENTION OR IMPRISONMENT

- Standard Minimum Rules for the Treatment of Prisoners
- Basic Principles for the Treatment of Prisoners
- Body of Principles for the Protection of All Persons under Any Form of Detention or Imprisonment
- United Nations Rules for the Protection of Juveniles Deprived of their Liberty
- Declaration on the Protection of All Persons from Being Subjected to Torture and Other Cruel, Inhuman or Degrading Treatment or Punishment
- Convention against Torture and Other Cruel, Inhuman or Degrading Treatment or Punishment (CAT)

- Optional Protocol to the Convention against Torture and Other Cruel, Inhuman or Degrading Treatment or Punishment (OPCAT)
- Principles of Medical Ethics relevant to the Role of Health Personnel, particularly Physicians, in the Protection of Prisoners and Detainees against Torture and Other Cruel, Inhuman or Degrading Treatment or Punishment
- Principles on the Effective Investigation and Documentation of Torture and Other Cruel, Inhuman or Degrading Treatment or Punishment
- Safeguards guaranteeing protection of the rights of those facing the death penalty
- Code of Conduct for Law Enforcement Officials
- Basic Principles on the Use of Force and Firearms by Law Enforcement Officials
- United Nations Standard Minimum Rules for Non-custodial Measures (The Tokyo Rules)
- United Nations Standard Minimum Rules for the Administration of Juvenile Justice (The Beijing Rules)
- Guidelines for Action on Children in the Criminal Justice System
- United Nations Guidelines for the Prevention of Juvenile Delinquency (The Riyadh Guidelines)
- Declaration of Basic Principles of Justice for Victims of Crime and Abuse of Power
- Basic Principles on the Independence of the Judiciary
- Basic Principles on the Role of Lawyers
- Guidelines on the Role of Prosecutors
- Principles on the Effective Prevention and Investigation of Extra-legal, Arbitrary and Summary Executions
- Declaration on the Protection of All Persons from Enforced Disappearance
- Basic Principles and Guidelines on the Right to a Remedy and Reparation
- International Convention for the Protection of All Persons from Enforced Disappearance (not yet into force)

SOCIAL WELFARE, PROGRESS AND DEVELOPMENT

- Declaration on Social Progress and Development
- Universal Declaration on the Eradication of Hunger and Malnutrition
- Declaration on the Use of Scientific and Technological Progress in the Interests of Peace and for the Benefit of Mankind
- Declaration on the Right of Peoples to Peace
- Declaration on the Right to Development
- Universal Declaration on the Human Genome and Human Rights
- Universal Declaration on Cultural Diversity

PROMOTION AND PROTECTION OF HUMAN RIGHTS

- Principles relating to the status of national institutions (The Paris Principles)
- Declaration on the Right and Responsibility of Individuals, Groups and Organs of Society to Promote and Protect Universally Recognized Human Rights and Fundamental Freedoms

MARRIAGE

- Convention on Consent to Marriage, Minimum Age for Marriage and Registration of Marriages
- Recommendation on Consent to Marriage, Minimum Age for Marriage and Registration of Marriages

RIGHT TO HEALTH

- Declaration of Commitment on HIV/AIDS

RIGHT TO WORK AND TO FAIR CONDITIONS OF EMPLOYMENT

- Employment Policy Convention, 1964 (No. 122)

FREEDOM OF ASSOCIATION

- Freedom of Association and Protection of the Right to Organise Convention, 1948 (No. 87)
- Right to Organise and Collective Bargaining Convention, 1949 (No. 98)

SLAVERY, SLAVERY-LIKE PRACTICES AND FORCED LABOUR

- Slavery Convention
- Protocol amending the Slavery Convention signed at Geneva on 25 September 1926
- Supplementary Convention on the Abolition of Slavery, the Slave Trade, and Institutions and Practices Similar to Slavery
- Forced Labour Convention, 1930 (No. 29)
- Abolition of Forced Labour Convention, 1957 (No. 105)
- Convention for the Suppression of the Traffic in Persons and of the Exploitation of the Prostitution of Others
- Protocol to Prevent, Suppress and Punish Trafficking in Persons, Especially Women and Children, supplementing the United Nations Convention against Transnational Organized Crime

RIGHTS OF MIGRANTS

- International Convention on the Protection of the Rights of All Migrant Workers and Members of Their Families (ICPMW)
- Protocol against the Smuggling of Migrants by Land, Sea and Air, supplementing the United Nations Convention against Transnational Organized Crime

NATIONALITY, STATELESSNESS, ASYLUM AND REFUGEES

- Convention on the Reduction of Statelessness
- Convention relating to the Status of Stateless Persons
- Convention relating to the Status of Refugees
- Protocol relating to the Status of Refugees
- Declaration on the Human Rights of Individuals Who are not Nationals of the Country in which They Live

WAR CRIMES AND CRIMES AGAINST HUMANITY, INCLUDING GENOCIDE

- Convention on the Prevention and Punishment of the Crime of Genocide
- Convention on the Non-Applicability of Statutory Limitations to War Crimes and Crimes against Humanity
- Principles of international co-operation in the detection, arrest, extradition and punishment of persons guilty of war crimes and crimes against humanity
- Statute of the International Tribunal for the Former Yugoslavia
- Statute of the International Tribunal for Rwanda
- Rome Statute of the International Criminal Court

HUMANITARIAN LAW

- Geneva Convention relative to the Treatment of Prisoners of War
- Geneva Convention relative to the Protection of Civilian Persons in Time of War
- Protocol Additional to the Geneva Conventions of 12 August 1949, and relating to the Protection of Victims of International Armed Conflicts (Protocol I)

Protocol Additional to the Geneva Conventions of 12 August 1949, and relating to the Protection of Victims of Non-International Armed Conflicts (Protocol II)

11) Notes

1- William, C., 'International Law: an Assumption About the State System', *In World Politics, Vol.17, July 1965, pp.614-634*

Also see Henkin, Louis, 'Law and International Relations: States and Human Values', in *Journal of International Affairs*, Vol.44, Spring 1990, pp.183-203

2- Vincent, R.J., *Human Rights and International Relations*, Cambridge University Press, Cambridge 1986, p.129

3- For the EC policy making process see, David, C., *Politics and Bureaucracy in the European Community*, George Allen and Unwin, GB, 1970, pp.77-101. For the United Nations see, David, C., Coyle, *The Unbited Nations and How it Works*, Colombia University Press, New York and London, 1966, pp.78-94

4- For detailed account of the EC Human Rights Policy see, Alston, P., *The European Union and Human Rights*, Oxford Univrsity Press, 1999,

5- See, Miller, D. H., 'The Drafting of of the Covenent', Vol. II, G. P. Putnam's Sons,

New York-London, 1928, p.324, cited in Cassese, A., *Human Rights in a Changing*

Changing World, Polity Press, London, 1994, p.210

6- Ibid, pp.323-5

7- Cassese, A., *Human Rights in a Changing World*, Polity Press, London, 1994, p.17

8- Ibid, p. 19

9- According to the Article 5 of the Covenant such a decision required a unanimous vote.

10- General assembly Resolution 1514 (XV) Declaration on the Granting of Independence to Colonial Countries and Peoples, adopted on 14 December 1960.

For full texts of the basic international documents on human rights see, Brownlie, I.,

(ed.), *Basic Documents on Human Rights*, Oxford University Press, London, 1971

11- For a detailed account see, Karpat, K., 'Military Interventions: Army-Civilian Relations in Turkey Before and After 1980', in *State , Democracy and the Military*, Heper, M., and Evin, A., (eds.) op. cit. p.28

12- Dagi, op. cit. p.61

13- As of the end of 1998, the European Commission ended its role, which has now been supplanted through the 1998 reorganization of the European Court) The new European Court of Human Rights came into operation on 1 November 1998 with the entry into force of Protocol No. 11. On 31 October 1998, the old Court had ceased to function. However, the Protocol provided that the Commission should continue for one year (until 31 October 1999) to deal with cases which had been declared admissible before the date of entry into force.

14- For the text of the Convention and Explanatory Report see, Council of Europe's Text of Protocols CPT/Inf/C (89). For the additional Protocal see Council of Europe's Text of Protocols No: 1 and 2 CPT/Inf/C (93).)

15- See, Beitz, R. C., *Political Theory and International Relations*, Princeton University Press, 1979

16- For a detailed account of the different actions of the member-states on the see, Ugur, op.cit. pp.52-61

17- For a chronological account of this development see, Duparc, C., *The European Community and Human Rights, Office For Official Publications of the EC,* Brussels, 1992, p.13

18- Mower, Glenn, A., 'The Implementation of Human Rights Through European Community Institutions', *Universal Human Rights,* Vol.2, No.2, April-June 1980, p.50

19- Duparc, C., op. cit., pp.30-35

20- See, Karel, L.G.E, de Gucht, "Report on Human Rights In The World and The Community Policy on Human Rights for the Year 1987-1988, Doc. No.A.2-329/88, Luxemburg, Office For Official Publications of the EC, 1988. Also see, Duparc, op. cit.

21- These figures are based on information contained in the annual EPC reports on the Twelve's human rights activity. See, European Political Cooperation Documentation *Bulletin,* Florence, European University Institute, 1986-1992

22- The Permanent Mission of the Federal Republic of Germany to the UN, *Press Release,* New York, 17 May 1988

23- EPC, *Press Release,* Geneva, 22 February 1989, p.8

24- Amnesty International Working Paper, '*The Challenges of Change: Preparation for the CSCE Human Division Implementation Meeting*", Warsaw, 27 September- 15 October 1983", AI Publication, London, 1993.

24- 25- Lehna, Stefan, *The CSCE in the 1990s: Common European Home or Potemkin Village,* Vienna, Wilhelm Braumuller, 1991, pp.85-94

26- Personel Interview with MEP and Leader of the Socialist Group in the European Parliament, Pauline Green, conducted in her London office in December 1994. The interview was one of the series in which some other European politicians took part between December 1994 and January 1996.

27- Commission of the EC, 'Public Opinion in the European Community', *Eurobarometer,* November 1989, pp.21-33

28- According to Coates, the Parliament would vote on 5-6 resolutions on human rights issues in each part-session and two-thirds of its oral and written questions to the presidency of the EPC and the Council would concern human rights matters. See Coates, Ken, '*Human Rights in The World'* op. cit., p.54

29- For instance, the Copenhagen declaration of the European Council on 14 December 1973 stated that "...representative democracy, rule of law, social justice...and respect for human rights" were fundamental elements of the European identity. This statement was reaffirmed again in the Copenhagen summit on 8 April 1978 and in its resolution of 28 November, 1991. Also see Duparc, C., op. cit. pp.30-32

30- See Pijpers, Alfred E., 'European Political Cooperation and The Realist Paradigm', in *The Future of European Political Co-operation: Essays on Theory and Practice,* Martin Holland, (ed.), London, Macmillan, 1991, pp.8-35

31- For the EP resolution, see *Official Journal of the EC,* No: C 161, 20 June 1983, p.64

For the foreign ministers see, Doc. No: 86/230 in *European Political Cooperation Documentation Bulletin,* Vol. ", No:2, pp.57-58

32- *Official Journal of the EC,* No: C99, 13 April 1987, p.162

33- Personel interview with Pauline Green in December 1994

34- Ahmad, F., 'Military Intervention and the Crisis in Turkey', *Merip Reports,* No. 93 Vol.2, No.1 January 1981 also see, Dodd, op. cit. pp.50-52

35- See chapter 3

36- *Agence Europe,* No: 2977, 13 September 1980, p.3

37- *Agence Europe*, No:2979, 17 September 1980, p.3 Also see, *Official Journal of the EC*, Debates of the EP, No: 1-263, 19 November 1980, p.116

38- *Bulletin, EC*, No: 9/1980, p.52

39- *Bulletin, EC*, 12/1980, p.83

40- *Agence Europe*, No: 2978, 15-16 September 1980, p.3

41- *Agence Europe*, No: 2980, 18 September 1980, p.7 Also, Info Turk, *'Black Book on the Militarist Democracy in Turkey'*, Info Turk, Brussels, 1986, pp.342-343

42- *Agence Europe*, No: 2981, 19 September 1980, p.6

43- *Bulletin EC*, 12/1980, p.83 Also see *Agence Europe*, No: 2990, 2 October 1980, p.4

44- *Official Journal* of the EC, Debates of the EP, No: 1-263, 19 November 1980, p.136

45- The emergency aid was granted in 1979 when Turkey was in deficit in its payments. *Agence Europe*, No: 3029, 28 November 1980, p.11

46- *Bulletin EC*, December 1980, p.83

47- *Agence Europe*, No: 3037, 4 December 1980, p.10

48- *Agence Europe*, No:3037, 10 December 1980, p.4

49- *Info Turk*, op. cit. p.344-345

50- *Briefing*, 20 April 1981, p.6

51- Evren, Vol. 2, Milliyet Yayinlari, 1991, p.283

52- See Dodd, C, *The Crisis of Turkish Democracy*, Eothen, London 1990, p.62

53- *Official Journal* of the EC: Debates of the EP, 10 April 1981, p.277

54- *Bulletin EC.*, 5/1981, p.53

55- *Bulletin EC*, 6/1981, p.60 For the meeting in which NSC took the decision, See

Birand, M.A., *Turkiye'nin Ortak Pazar Macerasi*, (Turkey's European Community adventure), Istanbul, 1991, pp.418-421

56- *Bulletin EC*, 6/1981, p.60

57- *Official Journal of the EC*: Debates of the EP, 10 April 1981, p.277

58- *Official Journal of the EC*: Debates of the EP, No: 1-279, January 1982, p.58

59- *Official Journal of the EC*: Debates of the EP, No: 1-287, July 1982 pp.147-148

60- *Briefing*, 25 May 1981, p.22

61- See Chapter three, NSC decisions as legislative law.

62- *The Times*, 5 November 1981

63- *Bulletin EC*, 11/1981, p.55 also see *Briefing* 16 November 1981, p.11

64- *Bulletin EC*, 12/1981 and Dodd, C., op. cit., p.62 also see *The Times* 26 November 1981

65- *Keesing's*, 22 January 1982, p.31287

66- Birand, op. cit. p.425

67- *Bulletin EC*, 1/1982, p.42

68- Ibid

69- *Official Journal of the EC*: Debates of the EP, No: 1-282, March 1982, p.42

70- *Official Journal of the EC*: Debates of the EP, No: 1-282, March 1982, p.123

71- *Bulletin EC*: 1/1982, p.42

72- *Bulletin EC*: 3/1982 p.21 and Dodd, op. cit. p.64

73- *Official Journal of the EC:* Debates of the EP, No: 1-287, July 1982, p.140

74- *Bulletin EC,* 3/1982, p.44 and Bulletin EC: 5/1982, p.51

75- *Bulletin EC,* 7/8, 1982, p.67

76- Foreign Broadcast Information Service: Western Europe, (hereafter FBIS:WE) *FBIS: WE,* 1JUNE 1981, P.1

77- See, Council of Europe, *Human Rights Information Sheet,* Vol.1, No: 11, 1982, p.11 also see Info Turk, op. cit. p.352

78- Birand, op. cit. pp. 423-424, also The Times, 5 March 1982 Following the trial of

DISK (Revolutionary Trade Unions Confederation) leaders and demands for death sentences for 52 of them, the European Trade Unions Confederation called on the EC to suspend all trade and assistance agreements with Turkey in protest against the suspension of Turkish trade union rights.

79- *Bulletin EC,* 9/1982, p.49, and 12/1982, p.78

80- *Bulletin EC,* 3/1983, p.63

80- 81=Birand, op. cit. p.435

82- =For the support of the British and German MEPs in the Parliament see, Dodd., op. cit. p.63

83- ANAP Government Programme, Ankara 1983, p.56

84- For further information see, Ozal, T., *Turkey in Europe and Europe in Turkey,*

K.Rustem, Great Britain 1991, pp. 312-316

85- Info Turk, op. cit. p.146

86- Simon, R., 'Turkey', in H. Shaked and D. Dishon, (eds), *Middle East*

Contemporary Survey, Vol.VI, Tel Aviv University Press, 1986, p742

87- *Bulletin of the EC,* No. 1-1984, p.48

88- See, *Council of Europe,* Yearbook of the European Convention on Human Rights, 1985, p.155

89- *Info Turk* op. cit. p. 370

90- *Official Journal of the EC,* Debates of the EP, No. 2-325, April 1985, p.158

91- Ugur, op. cit., p.370

92- *Info Book,* op. cit., p.370 also *Official Journal of The EC.,* Debates of the EP, No.2-325, April 1985, p.158

93- *The Time,* 26 July 1985

94- For the statement of the Foreign Ministers of the twelve on human rights see, *Bulletin,* 7/8 – 1986

95- *Official of Journal of the EC,* Debates of the EP, April 1985, pp. 158-205

96- *Council of Europe,* Yearbook of the European Convention on Human Rights, op. cit., p.157

97- *Info Turk,* op. cit., p.380

98- *Hurriyet,* 28 October 1985

99- *Milliyet,* 17 December 1985

100- *European Parliament Working Documents,* Document A 2-117/85, 9 October 1985.

101- *Official Journal of the EC,* No. C 343/60, 25 october 1985. For debates before the resolution see, Debates of the European Parliament, No.2 –331/47-63

102- *Agence Europe,* No. 4192, 26 October 1985, p.3 also *Milliyet,* 25 October 1985.

103- Guvener, S., K., *Kizgin Dam Uzerinde Diplomasi: Avrupali olabilmenin Bedeli* (Diplomacy on the Hot Roof: The Price for Being European), Istanbul, 1989, p.303

104- *Hurriyet*, 28 October 1985

105- *The Financial Times*, 10 June 1985

106- *The Financial Times*, 27 November 1985, also see, Info Turk, op. cit. *Bulletin*, No.110 December 1985, p.4

107- The Parliament also gained the assent procedure in relation to enlargement. This, naturally enabled the EP to have the last say on enlargement.

108- Evren, op. cit. Vol .1, pp.133-134

109- See, Cayhan, E., *Dunden Bugune Turkiye Avrupa Birligi Iliskileri ve Siyasal Partilerin Konuya Bakisi*, (Turkey and the EU: Past and Present and the Views of the Political Parties on the Issue), Boyut Yay, stanbul, 1997, pp.254-270. Also see, *TBMM Tutanak Dergisi* (Official Journal of the Minutes of TGNA), D17.9.4.435. 22.12.1986 p.165, (hereafter TGNA Official Journal)

110- See the epilleque.

111- The Turkish Grand National Assembly (TGNA) voted for a partial amnesty bill on 11March 1986, which lifted the ban on the expression of opinion on domestic and Foreign policy by former politicians.

112- *The Times*, 18 February 1986

113- *Official Journal of the EC*, Debates of the EP, No. 2-342, September 1988, p.83

114- Debates of the EP, No. 2-341, July 1986, p.95

115- *The Times*, 21 June 1986 also *The International Hearld Tribune*, 21 June 1986

116- Ibid

117- *Agence Europe*, No.4389, 17 September 1986, p.10 also see Debates of the EP No.2, 346/132, 12 October 1986

118- Howe's statement, President of the Council of Foreign Ministers, in *The Times,* 17 September 1986.

119- Turkey received 10 million ECU as a special aid in 1986 which was approved in 1980 and later suspended. Another 20 milion ECU was transferred from the contributions of Denmark, Ireland and Britain to the second EC – Turkey Financial Protocal.

120- *Agence Europe*, No. 4389, September 1986, p.10

121- *Official Journal of the EC,* No.C 7/109 - 111, December 1986

122- *Agence Europe*, No.4451, 13 December 1986, p.13

123- *Briefing,* 29 December 1986

124- *Bulletin* No.123, January 1987, p.2

125- *Official Journal of EC,* Debates of the EP, No. 2-350, March 1987, p.123 and No. 2-353, June 1987, p.87

126- *Official Journal of the EC,* Debates of the EP, No. 2-353 June 1986, p.169

127- *Official Journal of the EC,* No. C190/119, 19 June 1987 for further details on the EP's debates on the issue see, *Agence Europe*, No4573, 20 June 1987

128- For the full text of the resolution see Ibid, pp.119-121 also see *The Guardian,* 23 June 1987

129- *FBIS: WE,* 24 June 1987

130- *Agence Europe* No. 4672, 3 December 1987, p.3

131- *Agence Europe* No.4684, 18 December 1987 also see *The Financial Times,* 16 December 1987

132- For Evren and Ozal statements see *FBIS: WE.* 17 November 1987, p.21, and 19 November 1987, p.12

133- *Thirty Fifth Review,* op. cit. p.127

134- *Ozal, Press Conference,* 16 September 1985, p.16

135- *Milliyet*, 28 October 1987

136- *Agence Europe*, No.4733, 29 February 1988, p.4 The Convention provided for the investigation of complaints about torture by independent experts and allowed for visits to prisons as well as police stations.

137- *The Guardian*, 12 January 1988

138- Ugur, op.cit. p.190

139- For further information on JPC meetings the library of the TGNA and the documentation centre for the JPC (Karma Parlamento Komisyonu) in Ankara and European Parliament International Documents PE 139/059 of 6 February 1990 also PE. 141/174 of 15 may 1990.

140- *Official Journal of the EC*. Debates of the EP, No.2-373, January 1989, p.90

141- Commission Opinion, op. cit.p.7

142- Ibid

143- Commission of the European Communities, 'Commission Opinion on Greek

Application for Membership', *Bulletin Of the EC*, Suplement, 2/76, p.6

144- Commission Opinion, op cit. pp.7-8

145- For detailed account see; chapter III

146- For example, three days after the referendum on the new constitution, the Turkish Foreign Secretary went to Brussels to explain the new situation in the country and asked the EC to reactivate the Association Agreement and the Fourth Protocol. The Turkish Foreign Minister had also previously passed the news of the reduction of the prison sentence given to Ecevit to the Commission during discussions on Fourth Protocol. This shows how internal matters despite the military rulers' public defiance, became an issue in Turkey's foreign policy.

For further discussions see, Dagi, (1997), Dagi, I., 'Insan Haklari ve Demokratiklesme' (Human rights and Democratisation), *Turkiye ve Avrupa*, (Turkey and Europe), in Eralp A., (ed.) Imge Ankara, 1997 pp.121 – 171

147- Akder, H.,'Turkey's Export Expansion in the Middle East, 1980 – 1985', *The Middle East Journal*, Vol. 41, No.4, (1987), p.555. For general appraisals of the military regimes trade performance between 1980 and 1983 also see, the annual reports of *Turkish Union of chambers of Commerce*.

148- For the discussions in the NSC, see Evren, *Memories* , Milliyet yay. Istanbul, 1990, Vol. 2, pp.411-416

149- Evren, op.cit. Vol. 4 pp.147- 209

150- Pridham, G., Politics of the European Community, Transnational Network and Democratic Transition in Southern Europe', in *Encouraging Democracy: The International Context of Regime Transition in Southern Europe*, Pridham, G. (ed.) Leicester, Leicester University Press, 1991, p.222

151- Karaosmanoglu, A., 'The International Context of Regime Transition in Turkey', in Pridham, (ed.), Ibid, p.171

152- Dodd, op. cit., p.64

153- Hale, W., 'Transition to Civilian Governments in Turkey: The Military Perspective', in *State, Democracy and Military in Turkey in the 1980s*, Heper, M., and Evin, A, (eds.) Berlin, New York 1988, p.161 and Karaosmanoglu, op. cit. pp.172 – 173

154- For example, in 1981, despite the advice of the Turkish representative to the Council of Europe, Semih Unver, the military rulers rejected a visit from a delegation of the Council of Europe feeling annoyed by the frequency of fact-finding visits with regard to human rights. However, due to diplomatic pressure from the European capitals, the military rulers had to reverse their decisions within a month and set a new date for the visit. According to the Permanent Turkish representative to the Council of Europe, at the time, diplomatic pressure of Western states on the military rulers made the visit possible regrettably, not the Turkish diplomats advise on the case.

155- See Evren op. cit. Vol.2

156- *The Times* 13 February 1981

157- See chapter 3 and Barchard, (1985), op. cit. pp.43-44

158- See Evren, op. cit. vol. 3, pp. 50-55

159- Evren, op. cit. Vol.2, p.245 also Vol. 3 pp. 47-118

160- Evren, op cit. Vol. 4 p.355

161- Dagi, I., (1997), op. cit. pp.121 – 171

162- *Briefing,* 21 September 1981, p.4

163- Evren, op. cit. Vol. 2 p.380

164- Evren op. cit. Vol. 3 p.47

165- Evren, op. cit. Vol.3 p.26

166- *Milliyet,* 9 November 1990

167- Government programme, *TGNA Official Minutes,* D; 17, Y; 1. 19.12.1983, p.83

168- *TGNA Official Minutes,* D; 17, Y1 22.12.1983, p.105

169- *TGNA Official Minutes,* D. 17, Y; 2, C; 11,16.12.1984 pp. 19-20

170- Sakallioglu, C., U., 'Dogru Yol Partisi' (True Path Party), Yuzyil Biterken Cumhuriyet Donemi, *Turkiye Ansiklopedisi,* Istanbul, Iletisim yay., 1996, pp.1254 – 1280 also see *TGNA Official Minutes,* D;17, y;49 C;35, 22.12.1986, PP.165-167

171- *TGNA Official Minutes*, D; 17, y;49 C;35, 22.12.1986, PP.165-167 39/

172- Kayhan, E., *Dunden Bugune Turkiye Avrupa Birligi Iliskileri ve Siyasal Partilerin Konuya Bakisi,* (Turkey and the EU: Past and Present and the Views of the Political Parties on the Issue), Boyut Yay, stanbul, 1997, pp.254-290

173- *The Times* 20 February 1986 Also see, Turgut Ozal'in Basin Mensuplarina Aciklama, Mulakat ve Konusmalri 1087-1988, T.C. Basbakanlik (T.R. Prime Ministry), Ankara 1989 (T. Ozal's Briefings, Interviews and Speaches to the Press) hereafter *Ozal Press Release*, 4 December 1985, p.30 – 31, also see Ozal's speeches, 14 December 1985, p. 48

174- *PACE Working Papers*, Doc. No:5391, 18 April 1985, p.5

175- *The Times* 10 June 1985

176- *Ozal, Press Release*, 7 January 1984, p.26

177- *TGNA Official Minutes*, D; 17, Y,4 C35, pp. 117 –118

178- *The Times* 6 January 1984

179- *PACE,* Official Report, 10 May 1984, pp.189- 190

180- For acknowledgement of the some European criticism as right see Ozal speach in Turkish Democracy Endowment, Bulletin, 1991, p.3 For improvement of prison conditions see *Ozal Press Release*, 31 March 1984, p.5

181 - See Amnesty International, *Turkey: Testimony on Torture*, AI publication, London, 1985. Also see, *Turkey: No Security Without Human Rights*, AI publication, London, 1996, pp.33-58

182- Turkish Foreign Ministry gave the number convicted for torturing from 1980 to mid 1985 as 105, see *The Times*, 26 July 1985

183- For detailed account of the discussions on the issue in the Turkish Grand Assembly See, *TGNA Official Minutes*, issues D;

17, Y, 4 C35, 1986 pp. 117 –118., D;17, Y;4 C;22,1985, pp.510-516 also Cayhan, E., *Dunden Bugune Turkiye Avrupa Birligi Iliskileri ve Siyasal Partilerin Konuya Bakisi,* (Turkey and the EU: Past and Present and the Views of the Political Parties on the Issue", Boyut Yay, stanbul, 1997, pp.254-290

184- Article 19, State of Flux, p.9

185- Evren, op. cit. Vol.5 p.59

186- Evren op. cit. Vol. 5, p.383

187- Ibid

188- Ozal, *Bulten,* p.15

189 - *Hurriyet,* 25 March 1987

190- *Ozal, Press Release,* 14 April 1987 pp.3-6

In the second half of the speech Ozal argued for the economic fitness of Turkey to enter the EC. For an opposite argument inside Turkey, See Gemalmaz, op. cit., p.59, who concludes that Turkey is far away from the basic standards of Western democracies because of continuation of post-1980 political juridical system which is responsible for these inadaquencies and is the basis of continuing violations human rights. Ahmad, (op. cit., p.216,) too claims that a full transition to democracy requires to amend major legal re-arrangements of the military regime; the constitution being the first one, political parties law, election law, laws on the press, trade unions, higher education, etc. Which were claimed to be restricting democratic rights and freedoms of Turkish society. For Dodd, (op. cit., pp.126-127,) Turkey fulfils two basic requirements of a democracy out of three; though civilian rule and free elections presence in the country, it fails in respect for human rights. This does not mean that Turkey does not recognise human rights in its constitution, but it includes many restrictions on their use, which leads to a limited democracy. Also see, Ozbudun, Human Rights and the Rule of Law, pp.l 98-202.

191- See FBIS:WE, 25 September 1987, p.14

192- *FBIS: WE*, 15 April 1987 also see *Milliyet* 15 April 1987

193- See *PACE Official Report*, 18th Session, 27 September 1989

194- Evren op. cit. Vol.5, p.62

195- Mr. Guzel was imprisoned for 1 year and prohibited from politics for life (in 1999) for his public speech about human rights violations and restrictions on free speech. For the text of the government statement see *FBIS: WE*, 28 January 1987, p.5

196- See Gemalmaz, M., op. cit. p.24

197- For the full story see Cemal, H., op. cit., pp.205-221

198- For detailed account of the argument see *The Times*, 9 September 1987

199- *Milliyet*, 30 May 1987, *Cumhuriyet,* 30 May 1987

200- See Evren op. cit. Vol.3, p. 313 also *FBIS: WE*, 24 June1987, pp.12 For Ozal's argument's see his statement, *Hurriyet*, 25 April 1987

201- *Ozal, Press Release*, 2 February 1989, p.70

202- *FBIS:WE*, 8 November 1989, p.45 The spokesman was Mr. Inal Batu

203- Evren, speaking in his official visit to London and Bon see *FBIS:WE*, 18 July 1988 p.12

204- For Turkish government argument see *Ozal Press Release*, Issues: 4 January 1989, 25 January 1989, 2 February 1989. For opposit argument see Amenesty International, *Turkey: Policy of Denial*, London, 1990 and M. Gemalmaz op. cit.

205- *Amnesty International*, Annual Report 1990, p.240

206- Dagi, I., in Eralp, A., op. cit p.169

207- Ibid

208- See Gemalmaz, M., 'Olum Cezasinin Ilgasini Amaclayan BM Uluslararasi Medeni ve Siyasal Haklar Sozlesmesinin Ikinci Secmeli Protokolu ve Turkiye'de Olum Cezalari Sorunu', *Insan Haklari Yilligi*, Vol.12, 1991

209- Akin Birdal (President Human Rights Association of Turkey) and Yilmaz Ensaroglu (President of the Organisation for Oppressed and People) saw the changes as only window dressings rather then aiming to improve the human rights situation in the country aiming to impress the European sand highlighted his concerns on long term government issue., Personal Interview, Ankara, 1996., also see *Amnesty International Report*, 1990, p. 138

210- *PACE official Report*, 27 September 1989, pp.501-507

211- Ozal *Press Release*, 9 April 1989, pp.150-151

212 - Dagi, I., op. cit. p.300

213 - Ibid

214 - Ozal, *Official Visits*, 14 April 1989, pp.118-119

215- The Opposition leader was Erdal Inonu, see, *FBIS:WE*, 29 March 1989, p.24

216- *FBIS: WE*, 19 December 1988, p.32

217- Official Journal EC, No: C262/127

SELECTED BIBLIOGRAPHY

Official Documents/Publications

a) Government of Turkey:

Basbakan Turgut Ozal'in Basin Toplantilari 7 January 1984-30 November 1987 (Press Conferences of Prime Minister Ozal), Ankara, Basbakanlik Basimevi, 1988.

Basbakan Ozal'in Konusma Mesaj, Beyanat ve Mulakatlari 13 December 1985 – 12 December 1986 (Premier Ozal's Speeches, Messages, Statements and Interviews), Ankara Basbakanlik, 1986.

Basbakan Ozal'in Konusma Mesaj, Beyanat ve Mulakatlari 1987-1988 (Premier Ozal's Briefings, Interviews and Speeches to the Press), Ankara, Basbakanlik, 1989.

Basbakan Turgut Ozal'in TBMM Grup-MKYK ve Siyasi Konusmalari 1988-1989 (Premier Ozal's Speeches to the MP Deputies and Executives), Ankara Basbakanlik, 1989.

Basbakan Turgut Ozal'in Resmi Geziler-Tesis Acilislari ve Toplantilarda Yaptigi Konusmalar (Premier Ozal's Speeches in his Olficial Visits and Meetings), Ankara, Basbakanlik, 1989.

Basbakan Turgut Ozal'in TBMM Konusmalari 1988-1989 (Premier Ozal's Speeches in the TGNA), Ankara, Basbakanlik, 1989.

Basbakan Turgut Ozal'in Yurtdisi Temaslarindaki Konusmalari 1989 (Premier Ozal's Speeches in His Foreign Visits), Ankara, Basbakanlik, 1989.

The General Secretariat of the National Security Council, 12 September in Turkey Before and After, Ankara, 1982.

Hukumet Programi 1983 (Government Programme), (Ankara, Basbakanlik, 1986).

T.C. Resmi Gazete (Turkish Republic Official Gazette), Prime Ministry Office, Ankara, (Various Issues)

Turkish Republic Official Gazette No: 17119

Turkish Republic Official Gazette No: 17188

Turkish Republic Official Gazette No: 12303

Turkish Republic Official Gazette No: 2304

Turkish Republic Official Gazette No: 17112

Turkish Republic Official Gazette No: 2932

Turkish Republic Official Gazette No: 2533

Turkish Republic Official Gazette No: 18221

TBMM Tutanak Degisi (TGNA Official Minutes), (Ankara TBMM Various Issue).

TGNA Official Minutes, D; 17, Y; 1. 19.12.1983.

TGNA Official Minutes, D; 17, Y1 22.12.1983.

TGNA Official Minutes, D. 17, Y; 2, C; 11,16.12.1984.

TGNA Official Minutes, D;17, y;49 C;35, 22.12.1986, PP.165-167

TGNA Official Minutes, D; 17, Y; 49 C; 35, 22.12.1986, PP.165-167 39/

TGNA Official Minutes, D; 17, Y, 4 C35.

T.R. Prime Ministry, 1987, *Ankara Agreement*, State Planning Organization, (Ankara SPO, 1987).

T.R. Prime Ministry, Additional Protocol, (Ankara SPO, 1987).

T.R. Prime Ministry Provisional Protocol Annex, (Ankara SPO, 1987).

Turkiye Cumhurbaskanligi Devlet Denetleme Kurulu, Demokrati-slesmeye Iliskin Inceleme Arastirma Raporu, Document No: B.01.0DDK-32-106, Date and Number: 21.11.1996 - 1996/8, Unpublished Report From the 'Presidency State Investigation Bureau' to Prime Ministry Office.

T.C. Disisleri Bakanligi (Turkish Republic Ministry of Foreign Affairs), Turkiye ve idam Cezalari

Konusunda, (About Turkey and the Death Sentences), Document No: ATUY/ 760.9951-141-05 Date: 25 January 1994.

b) European Community:

AB Komisyonu, *'1999 Aday Ulkeler Ilerleme Raporu', Avrupa Komisyonu Turkiye Temsilciligi (EU Commission,' 1999 report on the advancement of the candidate states', EU Comission Representative to Turkey), (Ankara, 2000)*

Commission of the European Communities, 'Commission Opinion on Greek Application for Membership', *Bulletin Of the EC,* Supplement, 2/76.

Commission of the European Communities, *Background Report,* ISEC/B91817, (4th June1987).

Commission of the European Communities, *the European Community and Human Rights,* Office For Official Publications of the European Communities, (Luxemburg 1993).

Commission of the European Communities, Bullettin of the European Communities.

Commission of the European Communities, Twentieth General Report on the Activities of the Commission, (Brussels, 1987).

Commission of the European Communities, XXIII rd General Report on the Activities of the EC, (Brussels, 1990).

Commission of the European Communities, Turkey and the European Community, Background Report, ISEC/B9/87, (4 June 1987).

Commission of the EC, 'Decision Setting Up a Prior Communication Procedure on Migration Policies in Relation to Non-Member Countries' in *Official Journal of the EC*, no. L217, (14 August 1985).

Commission of the EC, *Communication to the Council and the Parliament an Human Rights, Democracy and Development Co-operation Policy*, SEC(91)61, final, Brussels, (25 March 1991).

Commission of the EC, *Communication to the Council an Relations with Turkey*, SEC (90) 10 17/final, Brussels, (12 June 1990).

Commission of the EC, *Opinion on Turkey's Request for Accession to the Community*, SEC (89) 2290/final, Brussels, (20 December 1989).

Commission of the EC, *The Turkish Economy: Structure and Developments, SEC (89) 22901 final*, Brussels, (18 December 1989).

Commission of the EC: Ankara Office, *Turkey - EEC Relations: 1963-1977, (*Ankara 1977).

Council of the EC, Agreement on the Financial Protocol to the EC-Turkey Association, Document 64/739/EEC in *Official Journal of the EC*, no.217, (29 December 1964).

Council of the EC, Agreement on the Adoption of Common Position prior to EC-Turkey

Association Council Meetings, Document no 64/737/EEC in *Official Journal of the EC*, no.217, (29 December 1964).

Council of the EC, Regulation 1842/71 on the introduction of safeguard measures against Turkey, in *Official Journal of the EC*, no. L192, (26 August 1971).

Council of the EC, *Treaties Establishing the European Communities,* Luxembourg, Office for Official Publications of the EC, (1974).

Commission of the European Communities, *Commission Opinion on Turkey's Request for accession to the Community,* Sec., 89, No.2290, Final/2, (Brussels, 20 December 1989).

Council of the EC, *Treaty on European Union* (Luxembourg, Office for Official Publications of the EC, 1992)

Gucht, Karel L.G.E. *Report on Human Rights in the World and Community Policy on Human Rights for the Year 1987-88,* Doc. no. A 2-329/88, (Luxembourg, Office for Official Publications of the EC, 1988).

The Council of the European Community, Agreement Establishing an Association between the European Economic Community and Turkey, Official Journal of the EEC, OJ No: 217, 29.12.1964., 64/732/EEC.

The Council of the European Community, Thirty Second Review of the Council's Work 1984, (Brussels *1985).*

The Council of the European Community, Thirty Second Review of the Council's Work 1986 (Brussels, 1987).

The Council of the European Community, Thirty Second Review of the Council's Work 1 January – 31 December1987, Brussels, 1988.

EC-Turkey Association, 'Additional Protocol' in *Official Journal of the EC,* no. C113, (24 December 1973).

EC-Turkey Association, 'Agreement Establishing an Association between the European Economic Community and Turkey' in *Official Journal of the EC,* no. C 113, (24 December 1973).

EC-Turkey Association, 'Association Agreement' in *Official Journal of the EC, N*o. C 113/2, (24 December 1973).

European Parliament, 'Resolution on Human Rights Situation in Turkey' in *Official Journal of the EC,* Doc: A2-117/85. No. C343/60, (31.12 1985)

European Parliament, 'Resolution on Detention in Turkey' in *Official Journal of the EC, Doc: B3-154/90* No. C38/80, (19 January 1990).

European Parliament, 'Resolution on Human Rights and Community Policy on Human Rights' in *Official Journal of the EC,* No. C99, (13 April 1987).

European Parliament, 'Resolution on the Armenian Question' in *Official Journal of the EC,* no. C190, 20 (July 1987).

European Parliament, Committee on External Relations, *Report on the Recommendation Adopted by the EEC-Turkey Joint Parliamentary Committee,* PE 57.075/final, (7 March 1979).

European Parliament, Council and Commission of the EC, 'Joint Declaration on Fundamental Rights' in *Official Journal of the EC,* no. C103, (27 April 1977).

European Parliament Doc. No: OJ No: C 176, 13.7.1992, (Strasbourg 1992)

European Parliament Session Documents, Report, Doc. No: EN\RR\292\292616, (12 February 1996).

European Parliament Session Documents, Report, Doc. No: EN\RR\288\288462, (11 December 1995).

European Parliament Session Documents, Report, Doc. No: EN\RR\288\288461, (11 December 1995).

European Political Cooperation, 'Memorandum on the Action Taken in the Field of Human Rights by the EPC' in *EPC Documentation Bulletin, Vo*l.2, No.1, (1986).

European Political Cooperation, 'Statement on Human Rights' in *EPC Documentation Bulletin,* vol. 2, no.2, (1986).

General Secretariat of the Council of the EC, *Thirty Fifth Review of the Council's Work, 1 January – 31 December 1987*, (Brussels, 1988).

Official Journal of the European Communities, Information and Notices.

Official Journal of the European Communities, European Parliament Working Papers. (Various Issues)

Official Journal of the European Communities, Debates of the European Parliament. (Various Issues)

Presidency of the EPC, 'Memorandum on the Activities of the Twelve in the Field of Human Rights' in *European Political Cooperation Documentation Bulletin,* vol.2, no. 1, Florence, European University Institute, (1986).

Survey of the Main Activities of the European Parliament July 1985 – June 1986, Directorate General for Research, (1986).

Survey of the Main Activities of the European Parliament July 1987 - June 1988, Directorate General for Research.

The Unseen Treaty, Treaty on European Union, Maastricht 1992, Full Text of the Maastricht Treaty, David Pollard Publishing, Kent, 1992

c) Council of Europe:

Council of Europe, Yearbook of the European Convention on Human Rights, (1985).

Council of Europe's Text of Protocols CPT/Inf/C (89).

Council of Europe's Text of Protocols CPT/Inf/C (93).

Council of Europe, *Human Rights Information Sheet,*(various volumes).

Council of Europe, *Yearbook of the European Convention on Human Rights,* Dordrecht, Martinus Nijhoff, 1985.

Council of Europe, Human Rights File, Strasbourg, 1978.

Parliamentary Assembly of the Council of Europe, Documents' Working Papers.

Parliamentary Assembly of the Council of Europe, Official Reports.

Parliamentary Assembly of the Council of Europe, Official Report of Debates.

Parliamentary Assembly of the Council of Europe, Texts Adopted by the Assembly.

d) European Commission of Human Rights:

European Commission of Human Rights, European Human Rights Report, Vol. 4, Part 16, Vol.4, Part 16, (October 1982).

European Commission of Human Rights, The Yearbook of European Convention of Human Rights (1983).

European Commission of Human Rights, European Human Rights Report, Vol. 6, Part.22 (May 1984).

European Commission of Human Rights, Stock-Taking on the European Convention on Human Rights The First Thirty Years' 1954 Until 1984 (Strasbourg, 1984).

European Commission of Human Rights, Stock-Taking on the European Convention on Human Rights Supplement 1985 (Strasbourg, 1986).

e) Other Governments/Intergovernmental Organizations:

Country Reports for Human Right-Practices, *Report Submitted to the Committee on*

Foreign Relations, US Senate and Committee on Foreign Affairs, US House of

Representatives by the Department of State, (From 1982 to 1989).

OSCE Parliamentary Assembly, Report of the OSCE Parliamentary Assembly's Delegation to Turkey 28 April – 1 May 1997, (Ankara 20 May 1997)

US Department of State, *Turkey's Human Rights Practices 1995*, Yearly Report,

US Department of State, *Turkey's Human Rights Practices 1996*, Yearly Report.

Books/Pamphlets

Ahmad, F., *The Turkish Experiment in Democracy 1950-1975*, (The Royal Institute of International Affairs, 1977).

Alkin, E., 'Turkey and the EC', *Journal of Istanbul Chamber of Commerce*, Issue 20, (Istanbul, 1987).

Union of Chambers of Commerce and Industry Maritime Trade and Commodity Exchange of Turkey, 'Special Economic Report 1989' (Ankara 1989).

Alston, P., *The European Union and Human Rights*, (Oxford, Oxford University Press, 1999).

Amnesty International Working Paper, '*The Challenges of Change: Preparation for the CSCE Human Division Implementation Meeting*', Warsaw, 27 September- 15 October 1983", (London AI Publication, 1993).

Amnesty International, *Country Reports*, 1980-1990 (London 1981-1991).

Amnesty International, *Testimony on Torture*, (London, 1985).

Amnesty International, *Turkey Briefing Human Rights Denied*,

(London, 1988).

Amnesty International, *Turkey: No Security Without Human Rights*, (London AI publication 1996).

Article XIX, *State Before Freedom*, (London, July 1998).

Ataov, T., *Amerika NATO ve Turkiye*, (Ankara Aydinlik Yayinevi, 1969).

Barchard, D. (1985), *Turkey and The West*, Chatham House Papers, 27, (London The Royal Institute of International Affairs, 1985).

Balkir, C. and A. M. Williams (eds.), *Turkey and Europe* (London, Pinter Publishers, 1993)

Belge, M., *Sosyalism, Turkiye ve Gelecek* (Socialism, Turkey and the Future), (Birikim, Istanbul, 1989).

Beitz, R. C., *Political Theory and International Relations*, (Princeton University Press, 1979)

Birand, M. A. *Turkiye'nin Ortak Pazar Macerasi (Turkey's Common Market Adventure)* (Istanbul, Milliyet Publications, 1986).

Birand, M. A, *30 Sicak Gun (The 30 Hot Days)* (Ankara, Milliyet Publications, 1984).

Birand, M.A., The Generals' Coup in Turkey, *(London, Brassey's, 1981)*

Birsel, Ismet, *Avrupa Ekonomik Toplulugu ve Tiirkiye-AET Iliskileri (European Economic Community and Turkey-EEC Relations)* (Ankara, Disisleri Akademisi Yayinlari, 1983).

Beddard, R., *Human Rights and Europe*, (London, Sweet and Maxwell, 1980).

Birand, M. A., *The Generals' Coup in Turkey*, (London, Brassey, 1987).

Birand, M.A., *Turkiye'nin Ortak Pazar Macerasi*, (Turkey's Common Market Adventure) (Ankara, Bilgi, 1985).

Brownlie, I., (ed.), *Basic Documents on Human Rights*, (London Oxford University Press, 1971)

Cankorel, B., 'Turkish Economy in the European Community Context', *Economic Dialogue* No: 22, (September 1987).

Cassese, A., *Human Rights in a Changing World*, (London Polity Press, 1994).

Celik, E., 'Avrupa Insan Haklari Komisyonu'na Bireysel Basvuru Hakki ve Turkiye' (The Right for Individual Petition to the European Commission of Human Rights and Turkey), *Bahri Savciya Armagan*, (Ankara, Mulkiyeliler Birligi Vakfi, 1988).

Cemal, H., *Demokrasi Korkusu*, (The Fear of Democracy), (Ankara, Bilgi, 1986).

Cemal, H., *Ozal Hikayesi*, (The Story of Ozal), (Ankara, Bilgi, 1989).

Cousins, J., *Turkey: Torture and Political Persecution*, (London, 1973).

David, C., *Politics and Bureaucracy in the European Community*, (GB, George Allen and Unwin, 1970).

David, C., *The United Nations and How it Works*, Colombia University Press, (New York and London, 1966).

Davison, R.H., (1981), *Turkey: A Short History*, (England, The Eaton Press 1981).

Devereux, R., *The First Ottoman Constitutional Period: A Study of the Mithat Constitution and Parliament*, (Baltimore, The Johns Hopkins University Press, 1963)

Dodd, C, *The Crisis of Turkish Democracy*, (London Eothen, 1990).

Dodd, C. H. (ed.), *Turkish Foreign Policy: New Prospects* (Wistow, The Eothen Press, 1992).

Donnelly, Jack, *The Concept of Human Rights,* (New York, St.

Martin's Press, 1985).

Duparc, C., *The European Community and Human Rights,* Office for Official Publications of the EC, (Luxembourg, 1992).

Davidson, R. H., *Reform in the Ottoman Empire 1856-1876,* (New Jersey, Princeton University Press, 1968).

Davison, R. H., *Reform in the Ottoman Empire: 1856-1876,* (New Jersey, Princeton University Press, 1968).

Dodd, C., *The Crisis of Turkish Democracy,* (London, Eothen, 1990).

Dodd, C., *Democracy and Development in Turkey,* (London, Eothen, 1979).

The Economist Intelligence Unit, Turkey Country Report, No.2, (1986).

Eren, N., *Turkey Today and Tomorrow An Experiment in Westernisation,* (London, Pall Mall, 1963).

Eren, N., *Turkey, NATO and Europe,* The Atlantic Institute for International Affairs, (Paris 1977).

A Helsinki Watch Report, State of Flux Human Rights in Turkey, (New York, December 1987).

Evin, A. and 0. Denton (eds.), *Turkey and the European Community* (Opladen, Leske + Budrich, 1990).

Evren, K., *Evren'in Anilari,* (Memoirs of Evren) Volumes 1,2,3,4 and 5, (Milliyet Yayinlari, 1991).

Gemalmaz, M. S., *The Institutionalization Process of the Turkish Type of Democracy: A Politico-Juridical Analaysis of Human Rights,* (Istanbul, Amac, 1989).

Ginsberg, R. H., *Foreign Policy Actions of the European Community,* (Boulder, Lynne Rienner, 1989).

Gonlubol, M., *Olaylarla Turk Dis Politikasi*, Ankara Universitesi Siyasi Bilimler Fakultesi Yayinlari, No: 509, (Ankara SBF, 1982)

Gonullu Kuruluslar Yasa Taslagi (The Proposed Law for Non-Governmental Organisations), Tusev Yayinlari No: 11, (Istanbul, 1996).

Guldemir, U., *Kanat Operasyonu,* (The Flank Operation), (Ankara, Bilgi, 1986).

Gunver, S., *Kizgin Dam Uzerinde Diplomasi Avrupali Olmanin Bedeli*, (Diplomacy on a Hot Roof The Price For Being European), (Istanbul, Milliyet Yayinlari, 1989).

Harris, G.S., *Troubled Alliance: Turkish-American Problems in Historical Perspective 1945-1973*, American Enterprise Institute, (Washington 1971)

Heper, M., *The State Tradition in Turkey*, (London, Eothen, 1985).

Heper, M. and J. Landau (eds.), *Political Parties and Democracy in Turkey*, (London, Tauris, 1991).

Heper, M. (ed.), *Strong State and Economic Interest Groups: The Post-1980 Turkish Experience* (Berlin, Walter de Gruyter, 1991).

Hershlag, Z.Y. *The Contemporary Turkish Economy,* (London, 1998).

HRFT, *Treatment and Rehabilitation Centre's report 1994*, (Ankara, 1994).

Info-Turk, *Black Book on the Militarist Democracy in Turkey,* (Brussels, Info-Turk, 1986).

Insel, A., 'Turkiye Toplumunun Bunalimi' (The Crisis of Turkish Society), (*Birikim,* Istanbul, 1990).

James, A., *Sovereign Statehood and the Basis of International Society,* (London, Allen and Unwin, 1986).

Jones., P., *Rights: Issues in Political Theory,* (Macmillian, London, 1994).

Kabacali, A. '*Turk Basininda Democracy',* (Democracy In the Turkish Press), (Ankara Kultur Bakanligi Yayinlari, 1994).

Kayhan, E., *Dunden Bugune Turkiye Avrupa Birligi Iliskileri ve Siyasal Partilerin Konuya Bakisi,* (Turkey and the EU: Past and Present and the Views of the Political Parties on the Issue), Boyut (Yay, Istanbul, 1997).

Keane, J., *Despotism and Democracy: The Origins and Development of the Distinction Between Civil Society and the State 1750-1850,* (London, 1988).

Kinros, L., *Ataturk; the Rebirth of a Nation,* (London, Morrison and Gibb ltd, 1964)

Kilinc, U., *Turkiye Avrupa Topluluklari Iliskileri,* (Turkey-EC Relations), (Ankara, TOBB, 1990).

Kocabas, S., *Kuzey'den Gelen Tehdit: Tarihte Turk-Rus Mucadelesi* (The Northern Danger: Turkish-Russian Disputes in the History) (Istanbul,Vatan Yayinlari, 1989).

Kocabas, S., *Post Modern Darbe,* (Post Modern Coup), (Istanbul Vatan Yayinlari, 1998).

Kuniholm, B.R., *The origins of the Cold War in The Near East,* Princeton University Press, (Princeton 1980).

Lehna, Stefan, *The CSCE in the 1990s: Common European Home or Potemkin Village,* (Vienna, Wilhelm Braumuller, 1991).

Lewis, B., *The Emergence of Modern Turkey,* (Oxford, Oxford University Press, 1961).

Lewis, G., *Modern Turkey,* (London, Ernet Benn, 1974).

Mackenzie, K., *Turkey Under the Generals*, (London, Conflict Studies, 1981).

Mackenzie, K., *Turkey in Transition The West's Neglected Ally*, (London, Institute for European Defense and Strategic Studies, 1984).

Manisali, E., (1979), *Foreign Economic Relations of Turkey*, University of Istanbul Publications, (Istanbul 1979).

Mazlumder, *Turkey's Human Rights Problem: the 1997 analysis*, (Ankara, January 1998).

Owen, R., *State, power and Politics in the Making of the Modern Middle East*, (Routledge, 1992).

Ozal, Turgut, *Turkey in Europe and Europe in Turkey* (Nicosia, Rustem and Brothers, 1991).

Cassese, A., *Human Rights in A Changing World*, (Cambridge, Polity, 1990).

Pevsner, L.W., *Turkey's Political Crisis' Background Perspectives Prospects*, The

Washington Papers 110, New York, Praeger, 1984).

Robertson, A. H., *Human Rights in the World*, (ed.) (Manchester, Manchester University Press, 1989).

Robertson, A. H., Human Rights in Europe, (Manchester, Manchester University Press, 1977).

Robins, P., *Turkey and the Middle East*, (The Royal Institute of International Affairs, London, 1991).

Rustow, D., *Turkey: America's Forgotten Ally*, (New York, Council on Foreign Relations Books, 1987).

Sander, O., *Siyasi Tarih: 1918 – 1990*, (Political History: 1918 – 1990), (Imge Kitabevei, Ankara, 1991).

Schermes, H. 0., *The European Commission of Human Rights: From the Inside*, (Hull University Press, 1990).

Schlegel, D., 'Turkish-European Pragmatism', *Aussen Politic*,

Vol.37, No.4, (1986).

Shaw, S.J. and Shaw, E.K., *History of the Ottoman Empire and Modern Turkey,* (Cambridge, Cambridge University Press, 1977).

Schapiro, L., *The Government and Politics of the Soviet Union,* (Hutchinson, London, 1979).

Teson, F., *Humanitarian Intervention,* (New York, Transnational Publication, 1988).

Thomas, C., *New States Sovereignty and Intervention,* (London, Gower, 1985).

TOBB (The Turkish Chambers of Cornmerce and Industry), *Planli Donemde Rakamlarla Tiirkiye Ekanomisi (The Figures of Turkish Economy Under Planning Periods)* (Ankara, TOBB, 1990).

Torture File: 12 September 1980 – 12 September 1994, (Ankara HRFT, 1994)

Turgut, H. *Turkes'in Anilari: Sahinlerin Dansi* (Memories of Turkes: Dance of Falcons), (.ABC, Ankara 1995).

Turkiye-Avrupa Toplulugu Dernegi (Turkey-EC Studies Association), Tam Oyelik Basvurusunun 7. Yilinda Turkiye-Avrupa Iliskileri (Turkey-Europe Relations on the 7th Anniversary of the *Membership Application,* (Ankara, Turkiye-Avrupa Toplulugu Dernegi, 1994).

Sencer, M., *Bireysel Basvuru Hakki,* (The Right for Individual Petition), (Ankara, Insan Hakiari Dernegi, 1987).

Shaw, J. S., and Shaw, E.K., *History of the Ottoman Empire and Modern Turkey: The Rise of Modern Turkey,* (Cambridge University Press, London 1977).

Ugur, M., *The European Union and Turkey: an Anchor/Credibility Dilemma,* Ashgate and USA, 1999.

Uskul, Z., *Siyaset ve Asker* (The Military and Politics), (Imge, Ankara, 1997)

Vali, F., *Bridge Across the Boshporus: The Foreign Policy of Turkey*, (Baltimore, The Johns Hopkins University Press, 1971).

Vincent, R. J., *Human Rights and International Relations,* (Cambridge, Cambridge University Press, 1986).

Vincent, R. J. *Human Rights and International Relations* (Cambridge, Cambridge University Press, 1986).

Wallace, H., Wallace, W. and Webb, C. (eds.), *Policy-Making in the European Community* (Chichester, John Wiley & Sons, 1987).

Waltz, K. N., *The Theory of International Politics,* (Reading, Mass: Addison Wesley, 1979).

Weiker, W.F., *The Modernization of Turkey: from Ataturk to the Present Day*, (USA Holmes and Meir Publishers, 1982)

Zurcher, Erik J. *Turkey: A Modern History* (London, I.B. Tauris & Co., 1993).

Articles

Ahmad, F., 'Military Intervention and the Crisis in Turkey', *Merip Reports*, No. 93 Vol.2, No.1 (January 1981).

Ahmad, F., 'The Transition to Democracy in Turkey', Third World Quarterly, Vol.7, No.7, (1985).

Akder, H., 'Turkey's Export Expansion in the Middle East, 1980-1985',The Middle East Journal, Vol.41, No.4, (1 987).

Akillioglu, T., 'Iskencenin, Insanlik Disi, Asagilayici, Zalimce Davranislarin Onlenmesi' (Prevention of Torture, Inhumane and Degrading Treatment), *Insan Hakialari Yilligi, Vol.10 - II, (1988-1989).*

Amnesty International, 'The Challenges of Change: Preparation for the CSCE Human Dimension Implementation Meeting: Warsaw, 27 September - 15 October 1993' (Working Paper) (London, August 1993).

Bagci, H., 'Turk Dis ve Guvenlik Politikalarinin Yeni Opsiyonlari Cercevesinde Avrupa ve Balkanlar' (Europe and the Balkans in the Context of the new Options for Turkish Foreign and Defence Policies), *Forum,* Vol.13, No.282, (1992).

Bahceli, T.S. 'Turkey and the EC: The Straits of Association', *Journal of European Integration*, 3, No.2, (1980).

Barchard, David, 'Turkey and Europe', *Turkish Review Quarterly Digest*, Vol.3, No: 17, (Autumn 1989).

Barchard, D., 'Turkey's Troubled Prospect', *The World Today,* (June 1990).

Bendix, Reinhard, 'State, Legimation, and civil Society', *Telos*, No:86, (1990).

Bilge, S., 'Insan Haklari ve Turkiye' (Human Rights and Turkey), *Ankara Barosu Dergisi*, Vol.46, No.2, (1989).

Birand, M. A. 'A Turkish View of Greek-Turkish Relations' *Journal of Political and Military Sociology*, Vol. 16, (1988).

Bourguignon, R. 'The History of the Association Agreement between Turkey and the European Community' in A. Evin and G. Denton (eds.), *Turkey and the European Community* (Opladen, Leske and Budrich, 1990

Bozer, A., 'Turkey's Relations and Prospects with the European Community' in *Turkish Review,* vol.2, no.3, Spring 1987.

Brown, J., 'The Military and Society: The Turkish Case', *Middle Eastern Studies,* Vol.25, No.3, (1989).

Brown, H. J., 'Turkey: A Foreign Policy in Flux', *Rust Journal* Vol.127, (June1982).

Bull, H., 'Human Rights and World Politics', in R. Pettman (ed.), *Moral Claims in World Affairs,* (London, Croom Helm,

1979).

Caha, Omer, '1980 Sonrasi Turkiye'sinde Sivil Toplum Arayislari (Civil Society in Turkey after1980', *Yeni Turkiye (New Turkey)*, (Ankara, November-December 1997).

Cayhan, E., *Dunden Bugune Turkiye Avrupa Birligi Iliskileri ve Siyasal Partilerin Konuya Bakisi,*(Turkey and the EU: Past and Present and the Views of the Political Parties on the Issue), (Istanbul Boyut Yay, 1997).

Cendrowicz, M. 'The European Community and Turkey: Looking Backwards, Looking Forwards' in C. H. Dodd (ed.), *Turkish Foreign Policy: New Prospects* (Wistow, The Eothen Press, 1992),

Dagi, I., 'Insan Haklari ve Demokratiklesme' (Human rights and Democratisation), *Turkiye ve Avrupa*, (Turkey and Europe), in Eralp A., (ed.) (Ankara Imge 1997).

Dagi, I. D., 'Insan Haklari, Uluslararasi Politika ve Kurt Sorunu' (Human Rights, International Politics and the Kurdish Problem), *Forum*, Vol.12, No.265, (June 1991).

Dagi, I. 'Democratic Transition in Turkey 1980-983: the Impact of European Diplomacy', in Kedouri, S., (ed.) *Turkey: Identity, Democracy, Politics,* , (London Frank Cass & Co Ltd., 1996).

Donnelly, J., 'Human Rights and Foreign Policy', *World Politics*, Vol.34, No.4, (1982).

Donnelly, J., 'Human Rights: the Impact of International Action', *International Journal*, Vol.43, No.2, (1988).

Dalacoura, K., 'Turkey and the Middle East in the 1980s', *Millenium,* Vol.19, No.2, (1992).

Ennals, M., 'Amnesty International and Human Rights', in P. Willets (ed.), *Pressure Groups in the Global System,* (London, Pinter, 1982).

Eralp, A., 'The Politics of Turkish Development Strategies', in A. Finkel and N. Sirman (eds.), *Turkish State,Turkish Society,* (London, Routledge, 1990).

Eralp, A., 'Turkey and the European Community in the Changing Post-War International System' in C. Balkir and Alan M. Williams (eds.), *Turkey and Europe* (London, Pinter Publishers, 1993),

Erdogan, M., 'Silahli Kuvvetlerin Turk Anayasa Duzeni Icindeki Yeri' (The Place of the Armed Forces in the Turkish Constitutional Order), *SBF Dergisi,* Vol.XLV, No.1-4, (1990).

Erguder, U., 'Post-1980 Political Parties and Politics in Turkey', in E. Ozbudun (ed.), *Perspectives On Democracy in Turkey,* (Ankara, Turkish Political Science Association, 1988).

Erguder, U., 'The Motherland Party', in M. Heper and J. Landau (eds.), *Political Parties and Democracy in Turkey,* (London, Tauris, 1991).

Evin, A., 'Changing Patterns of Cleavages Before and After 1980', in M. Heper and

A. Evin (eds.), *State, Democracy and the Military: Turkey in the 1980s,* (Berlin-New

York, Walter de Gruyter, 1988).

Finkel, A. and Hale, W., 'Politics and Procedure in the 1987 Turkish General Election', in A. Finkel and N. Sirman (eds.), *Turkish state, Turkish Democracy,* (London, Routledge, 1990).

Fouwels, M., 'The European Union's Common Foreign and Security Policy and Human Rights', *Netherlands Quarterly Review of Human Rights,* Vol.15 No:3, pp.291-324

Gemalmaz, M. S, 'Olum Cezasinin Ilgasini Amaclayan BM Uluslararasi Medeni ve Siyasal Haklar Sozlesmesinin Ikinci Secmeli Protokolu ve Turkiye'de Olum Cezalari Sorunu' (The Second

Optional Protocol of the UN Convenant of Civil and Political Rights, and the Question of Death Sentence in Turkey), *Insan Haklari Yilligi*, Vol.12, (1991).

Gozubuyuk, S., 'Avrupa Insan Haklari Sozlesmesi ve Bireysel Basvuru Hakki' (The European Convention of Human Rights and the Right for Individual Petition), *Insan Haklari Yilligi*, TODAIE, Cilt 9, (1987).

Gonlubol, M., 'A Short Appraisal of the Foreign Policy of the Turkish Republic (1923-1973)', *The Turkish Yearbook of International Relations*, Vol.14, (1974).

Gonlubol, M., 'NATO and Turkey: An Overall Appraisal', *The Turkish Yearbook of International Relations*, Vol. XI, (1971).

Gurel, S. S., 'Turkey and Greece: A Difficult Aegean Relationship' in Balkir, C. and Williams, A.M., (Eds.) *Turkey and Europe*, Pinter Publishers Ltd., (London and New York, 1993).

Guvener, S., K., *Kizgin Dam Uzerinde Diplomasi: Avrupali olabilmenin   Bedeli (*Diplomacy on the Hot Roof: The Price for Being European), (Istanbul,1989).

Hale, W., 'Transition to Civilian Governments in Turkey: The Military Perspective', in M. Heper and A. Evin (eds.), *State Democracy and the Military: Turkey in the 1980s* (Berlin-New York, Walter de Gruyter, 1988).

Held, D., 'Democracy, the Nation State and the Global System' in D. Held (ed.), *Political Theory Today,* (Cambridge, Polity Press, 1991).

Henkin, Louis, 'Law and International Relations: States and Human Values', in *Journal of International Affairs*, Vol.44, (Spring 1990).

Heper, M., 'The State, Politics and the Military in Turkey', *Comparative Politics*, (October 1983).

Heper, M., 'The State, the Military and Democracy in Turkey', *The Jerusalem Journal of International Relations*, Vol.9, No.3, (1987).

Heper, M., 'Motherland Party Governments and Bureaucracy in Turkey, 1983-1988', *Governance,* Vol.2, No.4, (1989).

Heper, M., 'The Executive in the Third Turkish Republic: 1982-1989', *Governance,* Vol.3, No.3, (1990).

Heper, M., 'The State, Political Party and Society in Post-1983 Turkey', *Governance and Opposition,* Vol.25, (1990).

Heper, Metin, 'The State and Debureaucratisation: The Turkish Case', *International Social Science Journal,* 125, (1990).

Hill, D. M., 'Human Rights and Foreign Policy: Theoretical Foundations', in D. M. Hill (ed.), *Human Rights and Foreign Policy,* (London, Macmillan, 1989).

Hill, D. M., 'Human Rights and Contemporary State Practice', in D M. Hill (ed.), *Human Rights and Foreign Policy,* (London, Macmillan, 1989).

Hindess, B., 'Imaginery Presuppositions of Democracy', *Economy and Society,* Vol. (1991).

Hoffmann, S., 'The Problem of Intervention', in H. Bull (ed.), Intervention in World Politics, (Oxford, Clarendon, 1984).

Karaosmanoglu, A., 'The International Context of Democratic Transition in Turkey', in G. Pridham (ed.), *Encouraging Democracy The International Context of Regime Transition in Southern Europe,* Leicester University Press, 1991).

Karpat, K., 'Military Interventions: Army-Civilian Relations in Turkey Before and After 1980', in M. Heper and A. Evin (eds.), *State Democracy and the Military: Turkey in the 1980s,* (13erlin-New York, Walter de Gruyter, 1988).

Keyder, 'The Political Economy of Turkish Democracy', *New Left Review*, (1979).

Kirkpatrick, J., 'Establishing a Viable Human Rights Policy', World Affairs, Vol.143, No.4, (1981).

Koc, V., 'Why Turkey Wants to Join The EC', *European Affairs,* Part 2, (1987).

Kuniholm, B. R., 'Turkey, and NATO: Past, Present and Future', *Orbis,* (Summer 1983).

Lewis, G. 'Turkey's Historical and Cultural Approach to Europe' in E. Manisali (ed.), *Turkey's Place in Europe* (Ankara, The Middle East Business and Banking Magazine Publications, 1988),

McFadden, J H., 'Civil-Military Relations in the Third Turkish Republic', *The Middle East Journal*, Vol.39, No.1, (1985)

Mango, Andrew, "Turkish Foreign Policy" in Ahmet Evin and G. Denton (eds.), *Turkey and The European Community* (Opladen, Leske and Budrich, 1990)

Mango, A., 'Turkey: Democracy Under Military Tutelage', *The World Today*, November 1983).

Mardin, 'European Culture and Development of Modern Turkey' in Evin, A., and Denton, G., (eds.), *Turkey and the European Community*, (Orient Institute, Opleden, 1990).

McFadden, J.H., 'Civil-Military Relations in the Third Republic', *The Middle East Journal*, Vol.30, No:1, (1995).

Miller, J. D. B., 'The Sovereign State and Its Future', *International Journal*, Vol.39, No.2, (1984).

Mower, A. Glenn Jr., 'The Implementation of Human Rights through European Community Institutions' in *Universal Human Rights,* vol.2, no.2, (April-June 1980),

Mower, Glenn, A., 'The Implementation of Human Rights Through European Community Institutions', *Universal Human Rights*, Vol.2, No.2, (April-June 1980).

Ozal, T., 'Turkey's Path to Freedom and Prosperity', *The Washington Quarterly*, (Autumn 1987).

Ozal, T., 'Turkey in the Southern Flank', Brassey's Defense Yearbook, (London, 1989).

Ozal, T., 'Turkey's Path to Freedom and Prosperity', *The Washington quarterly*,(Autumn 1987).

Ozal 'My Vision for Turkey' in *the Financial Times: A Survey of Turkey*, (20th May 1988).

Ozbudun, E., 'Development of Democratic Government in Turkey: Crises, Interruptions and Reequilibrations', in E. Ozbudun (ed.), *Perspectives on Democracy in Turkey*, (Ankara, Turkish Political Science Association, 1988).

Ozbudun, E., 'Human Rights and the Rule of Law', in E. Ozbudun (ed.), *Perspectives on Democracy in Turkey*, (Ankara, Turkish Political Science Association, 1988).

Penrose, T., 'Is Turkish membership Economically Feasible?', in *V*, Rustow, D. and Penrose, (eds) *Turkey and the Community, The Mediterranean Challenge:* Sussex European Papers No.10, (England 1987).

Pijpers, Alfred E., 'European Political Co-operation and the Realist Paradigm', in Martin Holland, (ed.), *The Future of European Political Co-operation: Essays on Theory and Practice*, (London, Macmillan, 1991).

Pope, N., 'Turkey and Turkic Republics', *The Independent Special Report*, (1 June 1993).

Pridham, G., 'The Politics of the European Community: Transnational Networks and Democratic Transition in Southern Europe', in G.

Pridham (ed.), *Encouraging Democracy: International Context of Regime Transition in Southern Europe*, (Leicester, Leicester University Press, 1991).

Rustow, D., 'Turkey's Liberal Revolution', Middle East Review, (Spring 1985).

Rustow, D., 'The Modernization of Turkey in Historical and Comparative Perspective', in K.Karpat (ed.), *Social Change and Politics in Turkey: A Structural-Historical Analysis,* (Leiden, Brill, 1973).

Sander, 0., 'Turkish Foreign Policy: Forces of Continuity and Change', in A. Evin (ed.), *Modern Turkey: Continuity and Change,* (Leske, 1984).

Sayari, S., 'Turkey: The Changing European Security Environment and the Gulf Crisis', *Middle East Journal,* Vol.46, No.1, (1992).

Sencer, M, 'Insan Hakiarinda Gelismeler' (Developments in Human Rights), *Insan Haklari Yilligi,* Cilt 12, (1990).

Sencer, M., '12 September and Its Aftermath: From the Perspective of Human Rights', *Turkish Yearbook of Human Rights,* Vol.9-10, (1987-1988).

Slater, J. and Nardin, T., 'Nonintervention and Human Rights', *The Journal of Politics*, Vol.48, (1986).

Spain, J. W. and Ludington, N., 'Dateline Turkey: The Case for Patience', *Foreign Policy*, Vol.50, (1983).

Soylemez, Y., 'The Turks in Europe: A Historical, Cultural and Diplomatic Perspective', in Manisali, E. (Ed.), *Turkey's Place in Europe*, MEBBM Publications, (Istanbul 1988).

Steinbach, V., 'Turkey's Third Republic', *Aussen Politic,* Vol.39, No.3, (1988)

Symposioum on International Protection of Human Rights', (Antalya 4 October 1991).

Tachau and Heper 'The State Politics and the Military in Turkey', *Comparative Politics*, Vol. 16, (1983).

Tanor, B., 'Political History 1980-1995', in Tanor B., and Aksin, S., (eds) *Turkiye Tarihi* Vol. 5, (Istanbul1995).

Tsardanidis, C., 'The European Community and the Cyprus Problem since 1974',

Turan, I., 'Political Parties and the Party System in Post 1983 Turkey', in M. Heper and A. Evin (eds.), *State Democracy and the Military: Turkey in the 1980s*, (Berlin-New York, Walter de Gruyter, 1988).

Turan, I., 'The Evolution of Political Culture in Turkey', in A. Evin (ed.), *Modern turkey: Continuity and Change*, (Leske, Schriffen den Deutschen Orient-Instituts, 1984).

Ulman, H. and Sander, 0., 'Turk Dis Politikasina Yon Veren Etkenler' (Determining Factors of Turkish Foreign Policy), SBF Dergisi, Vol 28, (1972).

Ulman, H. and Sander, 0., 'Turk Dis Poiltikasina Yonveren etkenler 1923-1968', *SBF Dergisi Vol. XXVI II*, (Ankara, 1972).

Vincent, R. J., 'Western Conception of a Universal Moral Order', in R. Pettman (ed.), Moral Claims in World Affairs, (London, Croom Helm, 1979).

Weiker, W.F., 'Turkey, the Middle East, and Islam', *Middle East Review*, Spring, (1985)

William, C., 'International Law: an Assumption About the State System', In World Politics, *Vol.17, (July 1965).*

Yesilada, B., 'Problems of Political Development in the Third Turkish Republic', *Polity*, Vol.21, (1988)

Zaim, Sabahattin, 'Turkiye'de Gonullu Kuruluslarin Son Yirmibes Yildaki Gelisme Seyri', (Development of Civil Society in Turkey in the Last 25 Years) (Ankara *Yeni Turkiye 1998).*

Periodicals

Agence Europe: (English Edition) (Luxembourg -Brussels).

Annual Reports of the EC-Turkey Association (Luxembourg, Office for Official Publications of the EC).

Annual Review of the Council's Work (Luxembourg, Office for Official Publications of the EC).

Bulletin of the European Communities (Luxembourg, Office for Official Publications).

Cumhuriyet (Turkish Daily).

Eurobarometer: Public Opinion in the European Community (Luxembourg, Office for Official Publications of the EC).

Europe Agence Internationale: (English Edition), (Luxemburg-Brussels)

uropean Political Cooperation Documentation Bulletin (Florence, European University Institute).

Foreign Broadcast Information Service: Western Europe, (FBIS: WE) (Various Issues 1980-1990).

Hurriyet (Turkish Daily).

Info-Turk Monthly Bulletin (Brussels).

Keesing's Contemporary Archives

Newspot Turkish Digest

Nokta (Turkish Weekly)

Milliyet (Turkish Daily).

Official Journal of the EC: Debates of the European Parliament,

(Luxembourg, Office for Official Publications of the EC).

Official Journal of the EC: Documents, (C Series) Luxembourg, Office for Official Publications of the EC).

Official Journal of the EC: Legislation, (L Series) Luxembourg, Office for Official Publications of the EC).

Newsweek (London)

The Economist (London).

The Financial Times (London).

The Guardian (London).

The Independent (London).

The Times (London).

Turkiye Gazetesi (Turkish daily)

The Observer (London)

Turkish Daily News (Turkish Daily-English)

Turkish Review

World Statement